CAMPUS SEXPOT

CAMPUS SEXPOT

SEXPOT

A MEMOIR BY DAVID CARKEET

THE UNIVERSITY OF GEORGIA PRESS

Athens and London

Published by the University of Georgia Press

Athens, Georgia 30602

Set in 10 on 16 Scala

Printed and bound by Maple-Vail

The paper in this book meets the guidelines for permanence

and durability of the Committee on Production Guidelines

for Book Longevity of the Council on Library Resources.

Printed in the United States of America

09 08 07 06 05 c 5 4 3 2 1

Library of Congress Cataloging-in-Publication Data

Carkeet, David.

Campus sexpot : a memoir / by David Carkeet.

p. cm.

"Association of Writers and Writing Programs Award

for Creative Nonfiction."

ISBN 0-8203-2755-7 (hardcover : alk. paper)

1. Carkeet, David—Childhood and youth. 2. Carkeet,

David—Homes and haunts—California—Sonora.

3. Novelists, American—20th century—Biography.

4. Sonora (Calif.)—Social life and customs.

5. Fiction—Authorship. I. Title.

PS3553.A688Z464 2005

813'.54—dc22   2005008514

ISBN-13 978-0-8203-2755-6

British Library Cataloging-in-Publication Data available

Portions of this memoir first appeared in the

Oxford American, *St. Louis Magazine*, and *River Styx*.

ACKNOWLEDGMENTS

I would like to thank the early readers of this memoir for their suggestions and support: Barbara Carkeet, Laurie Carkeet, Anne Carkeet, Carole Carlson, Ross Carkeet Jr., John Dalton, Roger Hart, Gwen Hart, Gerry Corneau, and Jessica Corneau.

For enriching my memories of these events with their own, I give special thanks to Roger Francis, Larry Leonard, Clint Paxton, Bob Finnegan, Colleen Finnegan, Al Martinelli, Jose Maciel, and Colleen Bill.

Several editors and writers have encouraged me in my nonfiction work, whether they know it or not: Suzannah Lessard, Joseph Epstein, Michael Caruso, Marc Smirnoff, Jeff Baker, Harper Barnes, Julia Hanna, Robert Hartwell Fiske, Robert Atwan, Glenn Stout, and Robert Bostelaar.

Many thanks to the Association of Writers and Writing Programs and the wonderful people at the University of Georgia Press.

CAMPUS SEXPOT

Linda Franklin had not been to bed with every boy in the junior college of Wattsville, but at nineteen she had known physical intimacy with a high percentage of those boys who knew enough to appreciate her amply endowed body.

As first sentences go, it's a good one. It treats Linda Franklin's promiscuity like a familiar subject, it shows a touch of wit in its sober contradiction of a preposterous assertion ("had not been to bed with every boy in the junior college"), and its categorical precision ("a high percentage of those boys who . . .") tells us we are in the hands of an author with a working mind.

But I did not see these strengths when I first read these words. I was fifteen years old, the year was 1962, and to me the opening sentence was a mounting wave that swelled to the climax of "amply endowed body." To a small-town boy in 1962, "amply endowed body" was like two large breasts slapping him in the face.

I had come home late from an out-of-town wrestling match to find my mother, her cheeks aflame, reading *Campus Sexpot*. It was without a doubt her first and last smutty book. She was reading it because everyone else in town was reading it, and they were doing so because its author was a former local high school English teacher who had vanished in the middle of the school year and gone off to write a sexy pulp novel set in our little mountain community. Many recognizable citizens, their names only slightly altered, misbehaved in its pages.

"This is terrible!" my mother declared from under her reading lamp, but she let me read it, and after I did, I burned it in the backyard incinerator. In those days, burning paper products outdoors was a regular practice.

Linda smiled and nodded to the many boys of her acquaintance as she walked down the aisle of the auditorium on the first day of school. Carolyn had saved her a seat in the section reserved for seniors.

The author's fictional milieu gives him a little trouble here. Having chosen to locate his action in a junior college, he nonetheless retains the trappings of the actual high school behind the story: assembly on the first day of school, incongruous designations like "seniors." How could an author capable of such a good opening sentence be this clueless?

At this point a girl turns to Linda and hisses, "Slut." Linda explains to her friend Carolyn that she went out with the "slut"-hisser's boyfriend the night before. But enough plot. It's time to learn more about Linda's body.

Linda was a pretty girl, standing only five feet three, gray eyes, amply endowed breasts, with a body that stirred longing in any man who looked at her.

The reader of page 2 is gratified to learn that no change has occurred in Linda's body since page 1. Once amply endowed, always amply endowed.

She had learned to use her body for her own gratification at an   𝓔
early age, for at fifteen she had been seduced by an older boy visit-
ing the mountain community of Wattsville. At first she had not un-
derstood what he wanted, but she had relinquished herself to him
in the back seat of his car in order not to appear a poor sport.

I read this now and think what I must have thought when I read
it in 1962: why didn't my dates ever worry about appearing to be
poor sports?

By the third night they spent together, the dam of passion within
her broke. She experienced a wild frenzy of delight, twisting and cry-
ing out with a barbarous abandon that frightened and at the same
time pleased her partner. After that, she spent most of her waking
hours looking forward to their next meeting.

Ah, yes — "the third night." According to the mythology of the
era, the third date was when it happened. But *what* happened,
exactly? Here no clothes are removed, no organs produced. An
alien reader of this text would think that earthly sexual intercourse
consisted of twists and shouts. That these circumlocutions could
arouse me, and I am sure they did, shows how little sexual stim-
ulation my world gave me — apart from the products of my own
fifteen-year-old mind, but nothing can come from nothing. Also
one has to wonder what this stoic visitor experienced while Mustang
Sally bucked in his backseat. Didn't *his* dam break too? But I didn't
ask these questions then. I was too busy learning about sexual response in the human female. This was my lover's manual, my *Joy
of Sex*. Drive, park, find your date's ignition, and turn her on.

When her seducer had to return to his home in the valley, she
found that a large number of boys of her acquaintance could provide
her with the physical satisfaction she craved.

It would have come as no surprise to the townsfolk hunched over this novel that it was a valley boy who deflowered Linda Franklin. On the golden mountaintops of Sonora, California, we knew that the distant fog below hid unspeakable evil.

Back to the assembly:

The curtain of the auditorium was raised and the principal, Harold Stoper, delivered his speech welcoming the students back to school. He uttered the usual meaningless platitudes.

"Crap," muttered Linda.

"Oh, Linda," protested Carolyn. "I wish you wouldn't talk that way."

"You're too nice," Linda whispered in reply. "Sometimes I think you're goody-goody."

Harold Stoper is really Harold Stoller, whose voice I associate with the delivery of the news, to me personally, of JFK's death in my senior year. It was during the lunch hour. I had been sequestered in a back room of the principal's office, taking a special exam for some interscholastic competition — like Linda's friend Carolyn, I was goody-goody. I had gone into that room wondering about the fate of my president, who had been reported shot and taken to a Dallas hospital. When I came out, exam in hand, Stoller piped without feeling, "He's dead!" I wanted to strangle him.

So, evidently, did the author of *Campus Sexpot*, whose name, I should tell you now, is Dale Koby.

"I want to introduce the new faculty members," the fat principal squeaked in his high-pitched, feminine voice. "First is Mr. Don Kaufield, who will teach English."

Don Kaufield stood up near the front of the auditorium, and the students craned their necks to get a look at him.

"That's our English teacher," Carolyn said. "He looks nice."

"Yes," murmured Linda. "I like him. Such broad shoulders." Don Kaufield at thirty had a healthy tan that suggested the outdoors, and clear brown eyes that were topped by a head of blond hair. He stood and smiled at the staring students, accustomed, after five years of teaching in another school, to the interested gaze of a youthful audience. His tweeds suggested a pipe, which in fact he fingered in the pocket of his jacket while he faced the students. He was muscularly built, with deep brown eyes that glinted with amusement as he met and returned the collective gaze of the assembled students.

This is one of my favorite paragraphs in the book. The best part is the way the narrator seems to happen upon the pipe in the tweed pocket: "which in fact he fingered . . ." You just can't beat that.

But how does Dale Koby measure up to Don Kaufield? In the Sonora Union High School yearbook of 1961, the author appears in two photographs. He is dark haired, not blond. Broad shouldered? Not obviously, and he looks short. His eyes glint with something like amusement, yes, but "zaniness" seems a better word. In one photo he perches cross-legged on his classroom desk, an open umbrella whimsically balanced on a shoulder. In the other photo, a lock of his otherwise swept-back hair dangles in a Sal Mineo curl over his forehead, and he stands before the blackboard glowering at the camera, eyes slightly crossed, his lips clenching a piece of chalk like an unlit cigarette. In sum, pipe-fingering Don Kaufield, in this introductory paragraph, is a cool observer of the teenage vale of tears. Dale Koby, in these yearbook photographs, is an imp.

Back in the auditorium, the first-day assembly breaks up, and the students begin to head off to class. As Don Kaufield passes Linda's seat, she introduces herself to him and joins him in the aisle.

6   She let herself be pressed next to him more than was really necessary as they walked up the aisle. Don was conscious of the sensuous warmth of the young girl pressing closely to him.

I know what Don felt. I too had a big-breasted girl press up against me at this high school. When it happens, it's an exciting time to be alive. I was at a school dance, standing in the middle of the floor. Perhaps a song had just concluded, and my dance partner had left me. At any rate, I was quite alone, with no jostling crowd around me. I suddenly felt a soft, pillowlike pressure against my back. I turned to find Marcia Labetoure, the contours of her *amply endowed* breasts obvious despite the heavy covering of burlap she wore. The event was a costume dance, though I'm not sure what she was dressed as. A sack of melons? She said, "Excuse me," and walked on, leaving me to my thoughts. A bit later, I tracked her down and asked her to dance.

It was a slow dance, ideal for my next move: I asked her to the prom. Before this night, we had never spoken to each other (she was a sophomore, I was a junior), but I must have felt the time was right to strike. I suppose I'm fortunate that I didn't propose marriage. My invitation to the prom made her jerk with surprise (not a pleasant sight; I had regrets already), and then she said sure. That settled, I asked her if I could give her a ride home that night. I had already worked out a detour that would take us to a remote parking spot in the woods. Her response was "Breasts." She probably said, "Yes," but I heard "Breasts."

The next thing I remember is my hand going to burlap and being removed, again and again. I tried several times, working her like a slot machine that wouldn't pay off. I figured that her private rule book required her to make a certain number of rejections, and if the payoff number was x plus one, only a fool would stop at x.

I also thought that if she had an absolute personal prohibition, as was beginning to seem the case, I might arouse her to the point where passion would break the barrier. But the magic paw wasn't working that night. I finally started the car, wondering where I had gone wrong. What were the rules? Was I allowed to feel her breasts only with my back? Should I have suggested we get out of the car so that she could press her breasts against my back again?

And what about the prom—the capstone social event of the year? For my sins, I now had a date booked with a virtual stranger who no doubt thought very little of me, as I did of her. What had I been thinking—that she would be so flattered that she would open her gunnysack for me? Had my invitation been that calculating?

When we reached her house, I walked her to the door (I was always polite that way) and made a bid for retraction. I said, "I don't think we're really cut out for each other." She blinked but said nothing. Her silence told me that she intended to hold me to the invitation.

For the next several weeks, I tried to break my foot. I would jump and land on it awkwardly. I tried dropping a brick on it, but I would pull my foot away at the last instant. I was too much of a coward, just no gumption at all.

I did what I had to do on prom night—put on my suit, let my mother attach my boutonniere to my lapel, and drove to Marcia's house. When she opened the front door, I almost sprang back in alarm. Her satiny blue dress was cut in such a way that the entire top half of her bosom was open for public viewing. My mind raced as I drove to the prom, where I got lots of elbow pokes from the guys. *Lucky you*, they said. But in the end, there was never any doubt about what I would do. When the prom was over, I drove Marcia straight home, accompanied her to the door, said, "Good night," spun on my heel, and walked away fast. In the wordless sexual community of adolescence, every gesture carries meaning, and my meaning was "I am not interested in your breasts. I haven't even *seen* your breasts. Breasts? Never heard of 'em, don't care if I ever do."

I don't know if the message was received. I do know that a few weeks later Marcia let it be known to some girls whose opinion I valued that she was "shocked and disappointed" when, after the spring costume dance, "David Carkeet got fresh" with her. Luckily the story spread only so far, then stopped. I heard about it from a grinning friend (himself not exactly blameless in these matters — his favorite phrase, and unattained goal, was "hands in the pants"); he relished informing me that Marcia had told the tale to Bonnie and Sandy, and I imagined that they too were "shocked and disappointed." But then, to my surprise, there was no further mention of it. Evidently my reputation as a "goody-goody" would be sullied no further. "David Carkeet got fresh" would not appear in the program notes for graduation, where, as student body president-elect, I would lead the pledge of allegiance to the flag. I was relieved that the story had faded, but I also felt betrayed. No, not betrayed, exactly — misrepresented. "What about prom night?" I wanted to shout to the world. "Doesn't that count for anything? My hands are clean!"

Let us return to our story. Linda Franklin has Mr. Kaufield in her last class of the day, a convenient arrangement, it will turn out. After class, she hangs around to chat and pretends to have missed the bus so that her teacher will offer her a ride home. He does, and just then her lover-of-the-month, Mike, sticks his head in the door to see if she's coming with him. She tells Mike she has a ride and

sends him away. There follows some banter between teacher and
pupil:

"You don't *usually* ride the bus, do you?"

"Nope," she laughed.

"But now Mike's gone, so you have to depend on me for a ride?"
he said wryly, running his hand through his hair. "You've very neatly
maneuvered me where you want me, haven't you, young lady?"

She smiled a saucy smile. Her shoulders sloped into an enticing
curve as she tipped her head sideways. "If you think so," she said
pertly.

"You need a good spanking for behavior like that," he said.

"Why, Mr. Kaufield," she said, her long eyelashes lowered. "*Who's*
***going to spank me?*"**

"Let's change the subject, Linda." He was sorry he had men-
tioned it. "Look, I'll meet you out by the faculty parking lot in twenty
minutes."

All novelists know that internal conflict is hard to render. The ap-
prentice novelist — which Dale Koby emphatically is — shows it by
having his character lurch abruptly from one pole to the other. Don
is obviously getting hot, what with all the saucy modifiers flying
around, and his passion elevates him to the high wit of his spanking proposal. But when he says, "Let's change the subject, Linda,"
the reversal is so incompetent that my mother's "This is terrible!"
echoes down memory's corridor with a fresh double meaning.

Linda was waiting for him by his car. She wore, besides her white
blouse, a white dirndl with large black roses on it, held out by sev-
eral stiff petticoats. A cumberbund accentuated her tiny waist. White
flats with sharply pointed toes completed the picture.

And a hell of a picture it is. Sometime between the classroom hunter and this meeting in the parking lot, Linda has gone off and joined the League of German Girls.

Don drives Linda home and pulls to a stop in front of her house, which is hidden in the woods. In a rural county, make-out venues are around every corner.

"Well, goodby, Mr. Kaufield," she said. "Thanks for the ride."

She turned to face him, leaning forward invitingly. Her skirts rustled with the peculiar sound of starched petticoats. He looked deep into her gray eyes, let his own wander over her lush young form, caressing each molded curve with his gaze. The silence of the trees surrounding Linda's house whispered their isolation. She took his hand and he pulled her to him, clasping her closely, crushing her firm young breasts against his chest. Their lips met, and hers opened to meet him. They clung for one long, rapturous moment, glued together by the passion both felt, then he pushed her from him roughly. She half lay in his lap, looking up at him.

"This isn't right, Linda," he said brusquely. "I'm a married man, and you . . . you're hardly more than a child."

Where to begin?

- Again, Don knows not what he wants, and the lurching becomes physical here, with poor Linda bearing the brunt of it.
- The tangible world is an enemy to a writer: it is so easy to get things wrong. If, in fact, "he pushed her from him roughly," how could the result be that "she half lay in his lap" without an intervening rebound that must be described?
- Behind every porno novelist is an aspiring real novelist, and the flashes of art are unintentionally poignant. Don parks the car. Linda leans forward invitingly. What will happen now? "Her skirts rustled with the peculiar sound of starched pet-

ticoats." This magnificent disharmony comes right out of the 𝑈 real world, where small moments of humanity intrude on our lust. It reminds me of the moment in *The Catcher in the Rye* when Holden Caulfield is distracted by the dress of the prostitute who comes to his room; he wonders about its purchase—did the clerk know she was a prostitute? J. D. Salinger and Dale Koby share a moment in their scaling of Parnassus. There is room on the ledge for both of them, at least for the duration of one sentence. But whereas Salinger will resume the ascent to artistic heights, Koby will plunge into the abyss.

Nothing further happens between Don and Linda. Today, at least, rocks will not be gotten off. Chapter 1 concludes with Don driving home and congratulating himself for his restraint. After all, he says to himself, "Linda might talk and thus get them both into trouble," and we certainly know what that's like.

Nelda Kaufield greeted Don with, "You're late," when he walked in the front door. Her tone was harsh, nasty. She was a trim, slender woman, dressed in a faultless suit, her make-up perfect. She offered no warmth. "It's almost as though you don't want to come home."

"I do want to come home," he said patiently. "Where are the kids?"

"Out in the backyard," she snapped. Her voice carried a tone of bitterness and sarcasm, the only weapons in her verbal arsenal.

We won't be spending a lot of time with Nelda. Her very name is a chastity belt, and it's clear that Don isn't getting much "warmth" at home. Still, he is a paragon of patience. After he checks on the kids outside, where he learns that Nelda has been mean to Susan (the older daughter, an early child unwanted by Nelda), Don comes back into the house.

"What's the trouble?" he asked Nelda.

"What do you mean?" Nelda replied, her nostrils flaring dangerously.

"Why put Susan out in the backyard and not let her in the house?" He slowly filled a pipe bowl with tobacco, placed the bit in his

mouth, and lighted it, sending blue-gray clouds of fragrant smoke
ceiling-ward.

"Is that what she told you?" snapped Nelda. Her pupils became pinpoints from her anger.

"What difference does it make? Did you, and if you did, why?" Don said slowly, puffing his pipe. He waited patiently for her answer.

"I put her out there with Betty because I just didn't have the strength to have any children around me for a while," Nelda said.

"They need your love and affection all the time, not just when you feel you 'have the strength' to endure them." He re-lighted his pipe, watching her carefully over the match.

Don basks in the self-satisfaction of many men in this kind of strife. Philosophically calm in the face of a hurricane of feminine irrationality, the man thinks, "Look at her. See her nostrils flare. Look at me, so patient. I am a saint. Where's my pipe?" This especially: "He re-lighted his pipe, watching her carefully over the match." This is no husband working on his marriage. It's Sherlock Holmes stabbing an inferior with his cold gaze. Don Kaufield, though fresh from a near-seduction of a student, brandishes moral authority. But is the scene more ridiculous for that reason, or for this one: why would anyone smoke a pipe during an argument like this?

I know all about pipes. I took one up in my junior year of college, adding it to my quiver of weapons of sexual conquest. The pipe was meant to be a corrective to my baby face. At twenty, my age then, I looked fifteen. (At fifteen, I looked eleven; at eleven, eight; at eight, six; I was baby faced even as a baby.) I smoked a pipe all through the rest of college and graduate school, the youngest—or youngest-looking—customer in pipe shops run by sallow owners, soft-spoken, throat-clearing men who lived in order to smoke, all now filling a fragrant grave, I am sure. I smoked Balkan Sobranie. I smoked Dunhill's. I smoked Borkum Riff. I smoked Sail Yellow but never Sail Green. I smoked Amphora, in a pinch. I smoked Latakia, a Turkish tobacco also used to boost Saturn rockets. I smoked so much that a college friend, reading a library copy of a French grammar of Middle English I had puffed over two semesters earlier, smelled my tobacco breath in its pages.

Did the pipe help me score? I can't say. I do know that it played a key role in the following incident, which took place nearly a decade after the action of *Campus Sexpot* and some two thousand miles to the east. In my first year of graduate school, I met an "advanced" young woman. I'm not sure what she saw in me. We shared a linguistics professor, though in different classes; the prof, fooled by a paper I had written, had mentioned me favorably to her, and therefore she found me worth exploring. Something like that.

We hung out a bit, went to a movie or two. Nothing sexual had happened, and I wondered if anything would. We were at her place one evening, lying on her bed and talking. She suddenly said, "I want to be touched." We were stroking each other as we talked, so I said, "I *am* touching you." "I want to be touched," she said again. After a few more repetitions, I got her meaning and went to work. Unfortunately, while I knew about how to get a pipe going, even in a rainstorm (pack tight and smoke with the bowl upside down), I didn't know how to do the same for a woman. I didn't know about touching. I remember the moment of failure well. There was an initial whispered *"Crazy!"* from her as I began my efforts, but I knew I was defrauding her. I remember thinking, "This is what women whisper when the guy knows what he's doing." I followed this fleeting triumph with some "touching" that lacked the benefit

of either experience or imagination. There followed a moment of
silence, then a brisk zipping up.

The woman then did a wondrous thing. She removed *my* pants and commenced to give me a blow job, my first ever. Crazy indeed. I recall it as a period of energetic but loveless commotion under a harsh ceiling light, and a full report must include the fact that I wasn't able to enjoy it completely. I enjoyed it. I just wasn't able to enjoy it completely. She eventually pulled away, put on a Bach concerto, and sat down with a massive volume of John Milton's verse. I knew then that the blow job was over.

I gathered my things to leave, ashamed of my multiple failures. Her parting comment: "How can a pipe-smoking devil like you know so little?"

It was a question for the ages, no doubt about it, and I mulled it over as I rode my ten-speed bike home, clouds of pipe smoke trailing mournfully behind me. On the one hand, the question confirmed that the pipe was indeed working as a sexual magnet. This was the first explicit confirmation I'd had after three scorched-mouth years. In this sense, I was on the right track. On the other hand, how *did* I know so little? The answer was the baby face. It had held me back, had made me self-conscious and slow to date in those crucial early-college years. I was a backward sexual recluse, a dormie for life.

A pipe to me is now a hateful thing in all ways. When Don Kaufield verbally stalks his wife, making his lawyerly distinctions and quoting her own words back at her superciliously, I want Nelda to knock that pipe right out of his mouth.

The couple's argument is put on hold by a long-distance call for Nelda.

Don watched as Nelda spoke briefly on the phone, her carefully

cared for face showing signs of strong emotion that were, for all the vehemence of their altercation, totally unrelated to it.

It's hard to describe a face shifting from one kind of unpleasant feeling to another, and Koby enlists some nifty syntax for the job here—good sentence number four in case you're keeping track. My advice to him, if he had handed me the manuscript for comment: make every sentence as good as this one. (Koby did do this, actually. He privately shared pornographic fragments from his pen with selected seniors in his final semester at Sonora High. Clearly a man with a career death wish.)

The phone call is about Nelda's father, who has just had a heart attack someplace faraway. This is the best thing that could possibly happen, both for the reader's interest in the novel and for Don's rocks. The author is so happy with this new development that he's got Nelda at the bus station before we hit the bottom of the page.

When the bus departed, Nelda was aboard it. Don took the children to a nearby restaurant for dinner.

There is a lot of doubling up of function in a small town, and Koby's got the geography just right here. The bus station in Sonora was really a magazine shop where the Greyhound bus stopped at the curb once or twice a day, and next door to the shop was the Europa, the town's most popular restaurant in the sixties. You could order milkshakes at the Europa, but it inexplicably lacked a mixer to make them and subcontracted their manufacture to the magazine shop/bus station. After ordering a shake, you kept a sharp eye on the door connecting the two establishments. A blockish, grim-faced woman would eventually emerge, scowling over your shake and then at *you* when you waved to get her attention. Next time you ordered a cherry Coke.

The Europa was where I took my first step into the larger world.
It was located at the bottom of the steep hill topped by our grammar school, and one day some worldly seventh-grade boys got the
inspiration to bypass the school cafeteria and charge down the hill
to the Europa for lunch. A few days into the routine, they invited
me. The idea of leaving the school grounds seemed so revolution-
ary that I could not believe it was not forbidden. It seemed equally
unlikely that a waitress would wait on a bunch of boys, treat them
with respect, and be treated respectfully in return. But from the
moment we left school, we were grownups. And the food! For the
same thirty-five cents that would have bought me a tiresome three-
course meal in the cafeteria, I bought a vast plate of French fries
and called it lunch. I reveled in the meal's imbalance. I knew that
my parents, if they learned of the adventure, would object in their
tired, rule-governed way. Dizzy with freedom, I floated through
that lunch hour and several to follow. The excursions came to an
end a few weeks later—I'm not sure why—but in that time, I was
a man among men.

Back in the Europa of *Campus Sexpot*, Don is about to have his
first encounter with Mike Allota, who is sitting at the counter.
Mike, as you have forgotten, is Linda's new boyfriend, the youth
whose offer of a ride Linda rejected in order to rustle her petticoats
in Don's Karmann Ghia. I've been avoiding Mike, an over-drawn
villain who lacks subject-verb agreement, but he will be important
to the story.

**"These your kids, Mr. Kaufield?" Mike asked, sitting down with-
out invitation. His eyes, Don noticed, were set too close together,
giving his youthful face a sinister, evil appearance.**

"Yes, they are," Don replied.

"Some of the kids were wondering if you was married," Mike said. "I guess this sort of proves it, don't it?" He nodded to himself, satisfied with the profundity of his observation.

Don looked at his girls with pride. "I've been married for ten years."

"That's a long time to be shacked up with one broad," Mike said, grinning at the license he allowed himself.

"Just a minute, Mike," Don snapped abruptly. "When you talk to me you find better words than those you just used. You're out of order."

"Okay, Mr. Kaufield. I just thought that a guy that goes chasing after Linda Franklin his first day in town, he must be pretty hard up at home." He arose and strolled away.

Don's buttocks are no doubt tightening here, possibly on the same vinyl seat where mine tightened, for I, like Don, once had a Europa confrontation with a hood. It was in my freshman year. I was sitting in a booth with some friends, giggling in my high-pitched way, only half-aware of a group of seniors behind me at the other end of the restaurant. Among them was Harvey Doff, whose drunken stagger into the restaurant a few minutes earlier, like everything else in my life, had filled me with a vague sense of dread. He was tall, gaunt, and stooped—"round-shouldered," as my mother would say, her words for the posture of a delinquent.

But Doff and I had no relationship, so I was surprised to hear from his end of the restaurant, during a lull in the giggling at my table, "I'm gonna go tell Carkeet to kiss my ass." Surely I had misheard this. Surely that wasn't Doff's voice slurring such an improbable agenda. But a glance across the table at one of my friends, his face a wild mixture of anxiety and delight, told me I had heard correctly.

Doff approached. I could tell from my friend's eyes, from the way they tracked Doff's progress over my shoulder. He came to a stop at my table. It was all unfolding with horrific inevitability. I stared down, afraid to look up.

"Is your name Carkeet?" Doff asked.

Odd as it sounds, I was flattered to be asked. *I am known*, I thought. *This fellow knows of me. I am a known figure.* Here we see the germ of vanity that is one of the wellsprings of authorship.

I looked up at Doff. "Yes," I said. I tried to seem eager for this new level of intimacy between us.

Time—or my fear—has erased from memory what Doff next said to me. This is a tragic loss to history because the exact words would clarify the nature of his beef. Round-shouldered hood that he was, did he resent me for being a goody-goody? Or had he been up before my father in juvenile court? (My father's position as superior court judge occasionally led to harmless comments from young toughs, like "Saw your dad this mornin'. He gave me hell.") I do vividly remember that I was rescued by a friend from band, big Bill Benson, whose round body was so well designed to carry a sousaphone that I wouldn't have been surprised to see him bearing one here in the Europa. Bill was with Doff, but he wasn't drunk. You couldn't be in band and be a complete hood—it just wasn't possible. Bill now joined us, asked Doff what he was doing, said I was his friend, and more. Bill handled it brilliantly, expressing amiable incredulity more than anything else. Doff slurred that if I was Bill's friend, then he had some pretty strange friends, and then he allowed himself to be led outside, where, Bill told me later, Doff burst out laughing, so he probably did not intend my death after all.

Doff and I must have seen each other many times in the course of the rest of the school year. Did he have any memory of this evening in the Europa? Did I think, *You were right to come after me, Harvey, for I am indeed contemptible?* Or did life just go on, each of us ignoring the other as we brooded in our separate miseries? In the yearbook for that year, every senior picture has a "Known for" next to the senior's name and picture. Doff was "Known for playing pool." Each senior also has a baby picture on the pages immediately following the regular senior pictures. It says something about Harvey Doff's life at home that no baby picture of him appears in the yearbook.

Back to *Campus Sexpot.* The next day Don Kaufield learns of an upcoming faculty party, and he will need a babysitter, what with Nelda being whooshed out of town and all. He asks Linda to sit, and on Friday evening he picks her up.

She wore a pair of tan riding pants which were so tight that they looked like they had been sprayed on. Don guessed that she wore nothing beneath them.

Just before he drives off to the party:

Linda gave his hand a furtive squeeze. "I'll be waiting up for you," she whispered.

Don drinks heavily at the party and roars back home in his Karmann Ghia. Linda greets him with a cup of coffee. They sit on the couch.

He looked at Linda. She tipped her head sideways, her lips offering themselves to his. He remembered the fire those lips contained, the promise her kiss held. He kissed her deeply, his tongue probing the recesses of her passion. She clung to him desperately, her young body alive with passionate fire, her nails digging tiny crescents in the back of his neck. Her breasts were crushed to him, and he could feel the blood pounding in her with a tempo to match the pounding

of his own. She moved against him expertly, arousing his desire to
fever pitch.

"God, sweetheart," he murmured when they finally broke apart.
"You're a passionate little bitch."

Don's delight in Linda's responsiveness, though dubiously
phrased, echoes a sentiment I've encountered in other fictional
renderings of male teachers seducing female students. The male
always seems happily surprised at the young girl's swift arousal.
Why? (1) The man gets off on his power over a younger person; (2)
the man gets off on the superiority of his skill to that of the girl's
pimple-faced peers; (3) more important, the man gets off on the
superiority of his skill to that of his own pimple-faced self years
before — he's correcting for his ham-fisted past; (4) finally, the man
who for some time has been "shacked up with one broad" more
than likely doesn't arouse his regular partner quite so quickly, so
he is genuinely impressed by the young girl's response. Lost in
a dream world of wish fulfillment and conquered regret, the re-
born man gives no thought to the irrelevant concepts of "good" and
"bad."

Back to the book's first sex. I'll try not to interrupt anymore.

He kissed her again, his hands working softly down over her
shoulders to the firm, round smoothness of her breasts. She lay on
her back, her shoulders in his lap, looking up at him.

"Unbutton me," she whispered, thrusting her breasts up at him.

His fingers were clumsy at the buttons, and even clumsier at the
hooks of her bra. She sat up and shrugged out of her shirt, revealing
her large, firm breasts. She slid to the floor and pulled him beside
her. She wore only the tan pants now, and they were so close to being a part of her that she gave the illusion of being nude.

"Touch me," she commanded, and he obeyed willingly.

His lips sought the erect nipples pointing saucily up at him. She writhed with pleasure at his touch, her passion mounting to match his. She let him stimulate her in this way for many minutes, reluctant to stop. She responded easily and well to his gentle touch.

He found her remaining zipper, and his guess of earlier in the evening proved correct. She slid from the tan pants much as a snake sheds its skin in the spring. He pulled her to him, fumbling with his own clothes. Then they were as one, blood pounding rhythmically together as they coupled closely. She pressed firmly against him, unafraid.

Minutes later she nestled her head on his shoulder as they lay there on the floor. Her long brown hair spread in a filmy net over his chest. She traced an idle pattern through it, enjoying the feel of his firm, mature body, so different from the youth she had known. More satisfying, too, because of his greater experience.

I hope you're satisfied. I'm not. In this book there will be no description of body parts below the waist. For the genital detail we're going to get, Linda might as well be a mermaid.

"Touch me," Linda says.

"I want to be touched," the grad student said to me.

Koby! Why didn't you teach me how to touch her?

The following afternoon, when Linda stopped by his desk, Don said, "Can you baby sit for me again tonight?"

Don adheres to the view once solemnly expressed to me by a college roommate: "Dave, never pass up a chance for a piece of ass." What Linda doesn't know is that Don, his wife still out of town, has deposited his two children at the home of a colleague for a few days. He has hatched a plan to get Linda alone again. He comes clean later, as they pull up in front of his house.

"Linda, there's something I should tell you." It sounded stilted, because he was nervous, afraid of her reaction. "Susan and Betty aren't here. I asked you to baby sit because I was reasonably sure that if I just asked you to come over, you'd refuse. If you want to go home, say so and I'll take you. I want you to stay, though."

"I guess I should say I want to go home, but I really don't," she said, taking his face in her hands and kissing him.

Good job, Don!

I too was once guilty of a fraudulent invitation for purposes of seduction. I was in the fourth grade, and my class was taught by a woman who spent the entire school year pulling up her bra straps.

Mrs. Wilcox would be lecturing us, going on and on, and suddenly a flash of white would slip into view against the flesh of her upper arm. We'd get an eyeful before she shoved it back up. It was a non-stop Victorian peepshow. Sometimes a strap adjustment required major intervention, and Mrs. Wilcox would leave the classroom to grapple with her garments.

That was when I would act. I was dreamily in love with Noel Swann. With my eyes fixed on her blonde head two seats in front of me, I would lean forward to the boy who sat at the desk between us and make this timeless request: "Ask Noel who she likes." Then I would raise my desk lid, hinged at the front. I needed that wall of wood between me and the determination of my fate. I would rummage busily in my desk, to all appearances a lad of vast industry, until my go-between, updated, would slam the desk lid down on my head, making Noel giggle before she whipped her blonde hair around and faced the front. Then he would give me her ranked list—coldly, bluntly. I was always second, after Johnny Alvarado.

This outcome was an early lesson for me in the attractiveness of bad boys to good girls. Johnny often rode the Bench—the wooden seat built into a corner of the central hall outside the principal's office for boys caught misbehaving. (No girl ever sat there.) I remember once, as we were filing into our nearby classroom, hapless Peter Mehen gave a benched Johnny the "shame, shame" gesture with his index fingers. Johnny bolted from the Bench—a jailbreak of sorts—grabbed a fistful of Peter's shirt, and said, "What did you just do? What did you just do?" Peter said, "Nothing! Nothing!" I watched, fascinated by the dynamics—a mere gesture could produce violence; a verbal negation of the gesture could be offered to restore equilibrium—but mostly thinking, *I'm sure glad I'm not Peter Mehen right now.*

Man has not pined for woman as I pined for Noel. On the play-
ground, I performed the Indian rub burn on her fair arms. I gave
her knickknacks that I won at the Mother Lode Fair—ashtrays,
mainly. I held her wallet-size school photo up to mine and made
them kiss, she in her Brownie outfit, I in my Cub Scout blues. One
night I played the piano over the phone for her. She hung up in
mid-recital, probably bored; when I called her again, she said that
the operator had told her to get off the line. Twenty years later, it
occurred to me that Noel had lied. But my mother was fooled. That
night, when I told her what had happened, she said that it must be
illegal to play a musical instrument over the phone and warned me
not to do it again.

On a Saturday morning around this time, I phoned a neighborhood boy to set up our regular exploration of the nearby
woods—there were pine trees to climb, acorns to collect, and old
mine shafts to throw rocks into. But instead of instantly signing on
to the plan, my friend told me he had invited a girl over to play with
him. I hung up the phone and stared into space, stunned. What did
this mean? What was going on?

But then I suddenly saw the possibilities. In fact, my friend's
idea seemed so inspired, so *right*, that I couldn't believe that he, a
year younger and demonstrably dimmer, had thought of it before
me. I went to my mother and asked her if I could invite Noel over
to play. She said no. I remember throwing only one fit in my life,
and this was the occasion. I dropped to the living-room rug and
began to writhe and cry. I had designs on this girl, a scheme so
vivid that it felt like something I had already done. I would get her
alone in the cool, dark garage, and I would kiss her. I would have
that kiss. The first step to get it was to writhe and cry on the living-
room rug.

My mother relented, and I phoned Noel, who asked her mother, who said yes. My sister would drive me there to pick her up. Everything was falling into place. On the way to Noel's house, I was as agitated as Gatsby on the verge of seeing Daisy. I had the details all worked out once I got her back to my place. Three key concepts formed my blueprint for seduction: FALL SILENT, JUST THINKING, and US.

First I would FALL SILENT.

Noel, intrigued by my silence, would say, "What's wrong, David?"

I would say, "Nothing. I'm JUST THINKING."

She would say, "What are you thinking about?"

I would say, "US." I don't recall further dialogue in the script. I must have reckoned that the sheer force of "US" would send her into my arms. This would all unfold in the garage, but how to get her in there? That was the first flaw in the plan. The second flaw quickly became apparent when, improvising, I abandoned the garage idea and initiated FALL SILENT in the house; she simply ignored me and went on doing what she'd been doing. Confused and resentful, I gave up and began wondering if my neighborhood friend was free to play now.

But then, at one point when Noel and I were playing with my brother, she took me aside to share an idea with me—some plan for tricking him. To get us away from him, she pulled me behind the Hopalong Cassidy drapes in the bedroom. There she giggled and outlined her idea, whispering in my ear. She was all over me, her blonde hair swinging in my face, her breath hot in my ear. Who knew it could be this good? Then she briskly threw open the drapes and resumed the game with my brother. When I emerged,

I felt as if I were stepping out of the orgasmatron in Woody Allen's *Sleeper*.

But later, when I thought about it, I realized the moment behind the drapes had meant nothing to Noel. She was *playing*, of all things. She certainly wasn't THINKING ABOUT US.

And still later—much later, after years of dating, putting the moves on women, storming them like Edmund Hillary scrambling up the south face of Everest, because that's what I thought they were there for—I realized that instead of becoming a fourth-grade seducer, *I* should have played too. I should have enjoyed Noel's company as she was trying to enjoy mine—trying and failing, no doubt. How much fun is a little boy who goes mute in order to put the moves on you in his garage? Perhaps this was the explanation for Johnny Alvarado's success—not that he was a bad boy, but that when he was with Noel he simply played with her.

The next year Noel moved with her family to Placerville, a gold-rush town so exactly like my own that the only point to its existence was to take her away from me.

Back in Don Kaufield's lair, Linda has some homework to do, so she sits down at the kitchen table with her schoolbooks and sends Don away into the living room, where he settles on the couch with a book. But then:

He became aware of her presence, minutes later, without seeing her. She walked across the deep carpet, at first her bare feet and ankles only coming into his view. She approached slowly. Her clothes had been left behind in the kitchen.

She stood before him unashamed, proudly flaunting her body. Her legs tapered with shapely curves to trim ankles and tiny feet.

Her buttocks were firm and well-rounded. Her belly was flat. Her breasts were large and firm, pointing upward with a pert insouciance that delighted Don, whether she was dressed or not. Her long brown hair hung in soft waves over her smooth, soft shoulders.

"Love me, Don," she said huskily, opening her arms to him fearlessly.

He took her then, savagely, clasping her to him again and again. She made little animal cries of delight as he probed for release from the pressure that drove him on. She sought nothing from him but surcease from her own driving passion.

The problem with the "good parts" of such a book is that we don't want to read anything else. Soft and bumbling though this passage is, we wouldn't mind if it went on longer. We know this about ourselves, and that is why smut has no literary status. Of *course* we'll read it. The question is where else can you take me? Can you hold my attention on a subject other than the one I think about around the clock already?

Afterward they cuddle, and Don tells Linda that she doesn't have to study for tomorrow's English test because she's already passed it. Linda says:

"I wish all my courses were as easy to pass as this."

"Now just a minute, young lady," he protested. "Think about what you're saying."

"Well," she replied. "It's easier than studying, and one hell of a lot more fun."

"Think of this with Mr. Pennymeade."

"Oooh!"

"And Mr. Roustland."

"Oh no!"

"And Mr. Warfield."

"Now *that* might not be so bad." Mr. Warfield was a young un-
married teacher of twenty-five.

"Sorry I mentioned him," Don said dryly.

"Mr. Pennymeade" is Mr. Pendleton, who taught me freshman general science. He was a kind and sweet man, a nerd before there was such a word, nervous, with nonstop dancing eyebrows. I wondered why teaching dolts like us would make him so nervous until I realized his eyebrows danced even when he walked across campus alone. In science, I sat across from the sexually obsessed Tom Shirley, who talked about blow jobs every day, told me about the photograph he had seen of the woman with a Coke bottle half inside her ("she must have been really loose," he said), and, because he had seen my prepubescent anatomy in the gym shower, said, "You'd be good for women who are really tight." When Mr. Pendleton demonstrated wave dynamics by holding one end of a long spring and shaking it up and down, unfortunately right in front of his crotch, Tom Shirley laughed and laughed. It was an ugly public laugh, a look-what-I-know laugh. I remember Mr. Pendleton nervously laughing along.

"Mr. Roustland" is history teacher Mr. Russell. He never taught me, and I knew him only as a tall, horse-faced man with a shit-eating grin. Our lives intersected once, on a band trip. Because I was such a dinky freshman, a highly desirable senior girl got it into her head to fool around with me on the bus. She whispered endearments and stroked my hair, my ears, and my neck while the cold bus chugged along. The word "cute"—a word I loathed—was on her tongue a lot. Her feelings? Probably nine-tenths maternal, one-tenth sexual. (I insist on that one-tenth.) As for me, I found her behavior unanswerable. I couldn't respond in kind, I couldn't ignore her, and I couldn't ask her to stop. All I could do was wriggle in my ill-fitting band uniform. Mr. Russell, the faculty chaperone for the trip, sat right behind us. A chucklehead, he was clearly unequipped to address the sadistic psychosexual drama in the seat before him. "Give him a couple years," he said to the girl, "and then watch out." I knew his meaning: "The boy has no manhood. Play with him at will."

"Mr. Warfield" is the handsome Mr. Warden, faculty advisor for the pep club, an organization that once enlisted my aid in the generation of schoolwide pep. It happened in the fall of my freshman year, in the very same WPA-built auditorium where Linda Franklin presses her breasts against Don Kaufield. A voice over the loudspeaker during a school assembly summoned me by name from the seated student body of eight hundred. I hurried on little-boy legs down the aisle, wondering what honor might be in store for me. I was whisked to a single folding chair at center stage behind the curtain. Whispers came from the wings. To the sudden blare of music, the curtain parted, and a swarm of popular junior and senior girls dressed as flappers rushed toward me and mimed adoration of my juvenile body as they lip-synched "Charley My Boy." While the audience screamed with delight, I blushed and thought about the faculty-student cabal that had engineered this spectacle. I could imagine the plan being hatched, under the sage leadership of the dashing faculty advisor: *Let's surprise the kid and see what happens.*

For me, every faculty member Koby-named in this chapter triggers a memory with a recurring theme. And no wonder. Take a look at the valedictions written in my yearbook at the end of my freshman year:

You're a real sweet guy and you've got a personality about twice your size. — *Evie*

To a little guy with great spirits. — *Russ Rolfe*

Small but mighty. — *Mike Pacino*

It sure has been fun knowing and playing an instrument with little oh you. — *Dick Baldwin*

Davey, A real fine featherweight wrestler that someday will be tops. — *Robin*

Best of luck to a BIG MAN. — *Jim Teem a wrestling buddy*

Lots of luck to a little guy who I'm sure will grow. — *Jim Guinn*

To a real clod. Start growing next year for football and you will do real good. — *Gerry*

Your gone to be good in sports next year only grow a little bit huh? — *Rog*

It's been a ball knowing you. Grow some next year huh? — *Jeff*

I have one word to say to you, "grow"!!! — *Bud*

When school began that year, I was four-and-a-half feet tall and weighed seventy-five pounds. When school ended in June, I was the same size. I was a cuddly human mascot, useful for all occasions. Not long after the "Charley My Boy" adoration in the auditorium, another summons came by public-address system, this one going to all the classrooms and calling me to the office of the student newspaper, edited by tall and skinny Verne Oliver. Verne explained that I had been chosen for a mistletoe-kiss photo for the Christmas issue, and he positioned me in the doorway under a festive sprig of the parasite in front of Lenette Young, a senior and the tallest member of the Tall Girls' Club. Lenette's face reminded me of Grace Kelly's flooring beauty in *Rear Window*. Everything about her made me want to say "a real dish!"

The photo spread was to be a three-shot sequence depicting ill-starred lovers trying to get together. I remember it well from the newspaper. Lenette towers over me in the first picture. She is on her knees in the second, looking unhappy on the hard, cold floor. No kiss yet. Our romance seems doomed. Finally, I stand on a chair. This puts me an inch or two above her. I remember wondering if I should kiss her on the cheek, but then I went for her lips. For some reason, I kept my jacket on through the whole sequence.

The last yearbook entry, commanding me to grow, came from the pen of Bud Castle, football coach of the "B" team on which I played. He will be introduced in *Campus Sexpot* a few pages ahead as "Bud Bastille, a broken-down softball pitcher," and Castle was in fact a windmilling softballer on the mound in statewide fast-pitch competition. He was a classic football coach, with a face that would go hang-dog when the team let him down and a repertoire of obscurities that he barked across the practice field: "You look like a bunch a monkeys with one thumb in your mouth and the other up your ass, waitin' for someone to yell *switch!*"

Castle treated me well, which is to say that he never once remarked on my size. In this he differed from our family doctor, who predicted permanent injury if I played football, and all the other townspeople and the students, who laughed in my face when they learned I was on the team. They said to me, "Whaddya do, run between their legs?" Everyone said this. There were no exceptions. I approached the daily practices with pure fear—not of injury, but of ridicule and general failure. I spent the afternoons at school before practices emptying my bowels until they were as clean as washed marble. In search of sympathy, one night I asked my father if he remembered feeling nervous before practices when he played football. He shook his head. "Only before games," he said. The discussion was over—not because he didn't care, but because whatever anxiety had me in its grip must have seemed too complicated to explore.

I "suited up" for just two or three football games in my freshman year. This was a high privilege because there were enough uniforms for only about half the team after the first-stringers. Suiting up meant donning a gold jersey with silken blue numbers as big as my back. It meant warming up with the regulars in the end zone and sitting close to the colorful action on the field. Suiting up also meant I might actually enter the game, a possibility that found surprising support from the stands. The B-team games were a preliminary to the A, or varsity, games, and the varsity players would watch until they had to leave for the locker room. They would often chant in their deep voices, "We want Carkeet. We want Carkeet."

Finally, it happened. I entered a game at the very end of the season for a single play. The crowd roared as I scurried out to the huddle. The second-string quarterback looked at me and said, "Big chance, Dave. Forty-six drive." I knew the play. The right halfback follows the fullback through the hole off left tackle, receiving the ball from the quarterback on the way. I was that right halfback.

The leaf in memory's album turns to a blank page, then turns again to a vivid image of the quarterback lunging for the ball, which for some reason is squirting across the grass. A long fellow, he looks especially gangly as he dives to recover the fumble. *My* fumble. When he put the ball in my stomach, it must have bounced right out. I remember thinking how heroic the quarterback looked as he went after that ball. I admired him. That's dedication, I thought. That's how the game ought to be played. How wonderful it must be to be normal and to play the game like that.

"May I speak to you for a moment, Mr. Kaufield?" Bill Alleyn's rich baritone voice broke in on the bitter thoughts Don Kaufield was thinking as he watched Linda Franklin leave the classroom with Vern Tolliver. For the past three weeks, Linda had ignored Don.

I know what you're thinking. You're thinking, "Who the hell is Bill Alleyn?" Bill was introduced in chapter 1 of *Campus Sexpot* as an innocent new student with "a rich baritone voice" and "a mature handsomeness." It was so quiet an introduction that I omitted it, and there has been no further reference to him in the book until the present moment. Get used to him—he will play a major role in the chaos still ahead. As for Vern Tolliver, if you recognized him as the fictional version of the real-life high school newspaper editor, Verne Oliver, good for you! You can play *Campus Sexpot* too!

Update: Don has really fallen for Linda. You'll recall that their second tryst got off to a crackerjack start ("'Love me, Don,' she said huskily"), but I didn't tell you how it ended—with Don suggesting that the two of them run off to Mexico together. The proposal baffles Linda almost as much as it does the reader, so she has pulled away. Now Bill Alleyn has awakened from the deep sleep into which he fell after chapter 1 and is stepping into Don's life.

"Sure, Bill. What do you want to talk about?" Don reluctantly chased thoughts of the passionate Linda from his mind.

"Well," the tall, blond boy said, "I don't know anybody in town, and there's a dance this Friday."

"I know. I have to chaperone it."

"I was wondering if you could suggest how I could find an opportunity to ask a girl to go with me. I sort of had one in mind."

"Oh? Who?"

"Linda Franklin."

Don looked at this tall, good-looking blond youth in surprise. "I'll see what I can do," he promised.

Imagine poor Don's chagrin. Here he's been shtupping the campus sexpot, has fallen in love with her to boot, and now blond Bill Alleyn, treating Don like the benevolent authority figure he isn't, requests his help in a match-up that is as bizarre as it is threatening to Don. This is exactly the kind of complication you want to happen in a novel. It's such a good plot turn that it makes me sad in the same way that "Her skirts rustled with the peculiar sound of starched petticoats" makes me sad.

Don arranges for Linda and Bill to be alone in his classroom so that Bill can speak to her in private. Later, Linda stops Don in the hall.

"Thank you," she said softly, smiling at him.

"For what?" said Don.

"He's nice. He's . . . well, different from the other boys I know."

"He'll be good for you, Linda," Don said softly. "He respects you, and that's important."

Let's set aside for the moment the strange shift in Don's behavior with Linda. Let's pretend he conked his head on a doorjamb and will soon be back to his old self. We'll focus instead on Bill Alleyn, a figure of some interest despite his unpromising chastity. Bill introduces goodness to *Campus Sexpot*, a concept fundamental to the adolescent social experience.

I was the youngest of three children. My sister, Carole, was born eight years before me, and the first word out of her mouth, according to the baby-book entry recorded by my mother, was the prophetic "good." She graduated first in her high school class, led the local Rainbow chapter, and infused the conservative Methodist church with a youthful passion from which it is still reeling. After college, she went to Yale Divinity School, postponed her career in order to raise two children to adulthood, then became a beloved pastor in the United Church of Christ. Her next life passage will be direct ascension.

Five years after Carole came my brother, Corky. Tortured by a mysterious rash in his early months of life, he needed to be held and rocked all through the night, and my father got much of the duty. To this day, my brother blames himself for my father's heavy drinking at the time, neglecting to consider the heavy drinking at other times. Corky was an adventurer as he grew up, and trouble had a way of finding him. It was trouble with a small *t*, but it seemed large, at least in our family. He played with firecrackers—outlawed in the Sierras—and made his own explosives from match heads. If Dad told him not to drive the family car past a certain point on Bald Mountain's uncertain dirt road, Corky would go three feet past the limit and immediately get stuck. At a young age, he chipped an upper incisor in a tumble, and, not long after, he chipped the adjacent one, creating a perfectly notched inverted "V" in his teeth that said, every time he grinned, "hellbent."

Like the silent stranger in a Western movie, I arrived in an atmosphere of suspense. Would I be a Carole or a Corky? I can imagine my parents watching my first display of willed behavior. Perhaps, belly down on the floor, I raised my head for the first time, spied a misaligned *Reader's Digest* on the bottom shelf, and straightened it. They would have turned to each other and smiled with relief.

Since I was a Carole—albeit one poisoned by testosterone—no deviance from perfection was possible. Moral lapses were treated not as products of the fallen condition common to mortals but as inexplicable aberrations. The David my parents knew did not do anything bad. And if he did, he never would again. Good boys got good grades. What's more, it was a general assumption that good boys who got good grades had no libido. While D-plus hoods rutted with C-minus sluts in the backseats of their hot rods, chewing on the bone of short-term gratification, straight-A brains supposedly sublimated their desire with hard study. Or perhaps they were already so sublime as to require no sublimation.

But I know that good boys feel lust, so I am tickled to see that Bill Alleyn has the hots for someone. That he has the hots for Linda Franklin illustrates a further principle: good boys lust for bad girls.

In sophomore biology, I shared a table with a sad, pale, stringy-haired girl from a province so remote in the district that she rode the school bus for ninety minutes each way every day. It's no wonder she was a mediocre student. Her reputation was even worse than her grades. Coarse boys were said to have explored her with their fingers in public—under trees on campus and on the long bus rides. These images made me zing with tension in biology, and fear issued into fantasy. She would make the first move, so it would be easy for me to abandon her once I was done with her. She would touch me under the lab table and suggest we meet somewhere, knowing that I could hardly take her on a regular date, given her reputation. We would get together on the football field late at night and have intercourse on the field — on the fifty-yard line, to be exact. That was my plan. It is often said that as we look back on our lives, we regret the things we *didn't* do. Not true.

There were other girls like her through the years, bad girls who haunted me, all attached to roughnecks who I imagined had their way with them, which is exactly what I wanted for myself. On the day of my graduation, during the afternoon rehearsal on the football field, bad girl Donna Linoberg sat on a folding chair with her skirt hiked halfway up her strong thighs while I stood nearby, going over the text of my salutatorian speech, "Whither We Go." Donna and I had never spoken, but for some reason she caught my eye, patted her legs, and said, "Sit on my lap." I looked at her and thought about the size of the explosion that would jolt Sonora High if I did that. I smiled and declined. It was a thrilling, impossible invitation. She might as well have said, "Come here and eat me."

Teenagers live in a world of instant, permanent labels, and "good" and "bad" were the favorites of my era. Before high school, most bad behavior was dismissible as child's play — the result of poor judgment or immaturity. Now we all faced a moral crossroads. Those who took the wrong fork would get into trouble with their parents, then the school, then the law, which meant they would end up before Judge Carkeet in juvenile court. Most kids took the good fork, but in the democratic stew of high school, solid citizens mingled with lawbreakers — in class, in the gym, at parties.

Anyone could end up being offered contraband, or as a passenger with a wild driver, experiencing the terror of reckless speed. In this regard, high school would be different from later life. As an adult, I never receive phone calls from crooks inviting me to join them for their next caper.

The good-bad dichotomy is cruel to both sides. Good children are expected to make it on their own. A document written in my father's hand illustrates this point—the "Parental Statement" portion of my application for a youth leadership award in my senior year. He wrote, "David early manifested a pleasing and amiable disposition," with a personality distinguished for its "equanimity" and "agreeability." David, in other words, has been maintenance free. But I didn't *feel* maintenance free, and I remember taking issue with the description at the time, but I kept this to myself, being so agreeable and all. The statement is written in bloodless prose, as if my father found the subject bloodless. Nicknamed Duke in his own high school and called Wild Man Carkeet in his yearbook, the judge showed traces of that reputed spirit whenever he described a youngster whose liveliness impressed him; he would say, "He's all boy." The words always made me wonder if I was boy enough for him.

Goody-goodies miss out on the fun. I knew this from the rare contact I had with a gang of boys less upstanding than me—this was a few years before high school, before the distinctions assigned us to different social circles. The group's unofficial leader was Johnny Alvarado, the persistent occupier of the number one position on heartbreaker Noel's list. With these boys, ordinary play had a way of shifting into a forbidden zone. On one occasion when I was included, a walk in the woods and fields turned into a bull-teasing adventure, followed by a cow-pie war. The high point of the day was the treeing of one member of the group, who clung for dear life atop a ponderosa pine, without ammo, while we bombarded him from below. He went home crying, which shook me a bit, but it still ranks as one of my best afternoons ever.

The same gang surprised me one Saturday with a phone invitation to play tackle football, without pads, at the high school. I remember my father grinning when I told him about the call, and I remember his interest as he dropped me off. The rough-and-tumble on the field fascinated me, but it was a mere warmup to the postgame crabapple war, waged at a wooden scorekeeper's tower on the sideline—a perfect fortress. Half the boys claimed the tower, and the other half, my half, besieged it. By the time we were done, the tower was stained and scarred, the hands of the timekeeper's clock were askew, and the ground was littered with exploded crabapples. As we left the carnage behind, I was breathless with joy. But I also wanted to cry out, "Shouldn't we pick up after ourselves?"

Or take Corky. He had all the fun, did only cool things. He and a neighborhood boy built a tree house in the distant woods large enough to play basketball in. He owned a black 1936 Ford pickup and tinkered with it in the lot above our house, soaking carburetor parts in shallow cans of golden gasoline—to clean them, he said, but to me the rich sight and smell were purpose enough. These aren't bad things, of course, but they require an independent, imaginative spirit that can also lead one into unorthodoxy. On Halloween, he and a gang of high school friends ripped an outhouse from its foundation and plunked it in the middle of the football field, penetrating the heavy janitorial guard line set up around the school. The next morning, the student body gazed at the result with a religious kind of awe. The most exciting thing I ever did on Halloween was throw a light bulb out into the empty street.

Corky fought forest fires in the summer. While I tended Calvert's Store for Men, he would roar down the main street atop a red state fire truck, waving when he zoomed past the store—Tom Sawyer off to conquer the world while prissy brother Sid straightened shirts. My father must have seen my brother as a kindred spirit—as a "Duke." When the time came for Corky's sex talk—I would get one later, but of a different flavor—my father gave him profoundly useful advice: "Some people say a rubber isn't good protection, Corky, but if you've got a good hard-on and get it on right, it works just fine."

But while bad boys and hoods have fun, they get a raw deal. They're underappreciated. One of the clearest class divisions in Sonora was between the homeowners and the renters. The latter lived on side streets, sometimes right off the main street, and it was a shock to me to see them walk up rickety wooden steps to a tin-roofed apartment over a store. I had always thought downtown was for shopping. I remember one of the renters, Allen Cardwell, a dresser so slick that if his hair wasn't working right for him he would leave school in midday. Allen was in my English class in junior year, and one day he gave a book report, standing tall before the class in his high-heeled black dress boots, all the rage in his crowd then. With his face buried in a page, in a voice made thin with self-consciousness, he read at breakneck speed. When he finished, he hurried back to his desk as if fearing arrest on the way. Gentle Mr. Wilkins urged him to speak a bit more slowly next time, reddening his face. The report had been sensible and informative, and I remember thinking what a fresh new person to hear from, what a triumph for him. But it was a fleeting insight, and no doubt within seconds I was back to my comfortable categories.

And there was Wally Enyart, a trumpet player in band and so not a complete derelict. Just a rebel, with a Friday-night floridness suggesting you might smell a forbidden something on his breath at the after-game dance. For our band director, Enyart was a source of alternating annoyance and amusement. One spring, at the annual competition of the state music educators' association, after our performance the director took us all aside and talked to us very seriously. He said he we had never played so well and he didn't care what the judges' scores were. (The scores turned out to be very good.) Of our performance of the theme from *Hansel and Gretel*, he said, "When I saw Enyart playing with his eyes closed, I knew something good was happening."

Enyart playing with his eyes closed. Let's add his name to the list of music-loving cutups, way up there, right after Mozart's.

Or consider Duane Mintzer, a zit-spackled junior. I didn't really know him, but nonetheless he regularly stuck his fist in my freshman face and said, "You're a little pimp." I was baffled by his hostility, but now I think I understand it. Duane had a girl-friend, big Ginny Bowen, and he was always entwined with her between classes. Whenever I walked by them, Ginny would say hi. I would say hi in my piping voice, she would laugh like the fat lady at the carnival, and Duane would say, "You're a little pimp." It was obviously hilarious to her to get a serious hi from such a homunculus, and of course I never let her down and always dutifully returned her greeting. But it wasn't this recurring sick routine that enraged Duane. What he hated was that I contaminated him. Duane wanted to be a man, and how could he be a man if I was part of his world, especially his football world? You see, Duane was

on the B football team, which consisted of freshmen and sopho-
mores and a few smallish upperclassmen, and this means he must
have been a short junior (I've arrived at his true probable size by
deduction; in memory he is large). Duane doubtless wanted to
be on the A team, the Wildcats—juniors and seniors who worked
out at the other end of the field every afternoon, in galling prox-
imity to the B team (the Wildkittens). Duane wanted to be a man
among men. Instead, he was a man among me.

I wanted to be a man too, Duane. Like you, I wanted to punch out
the little pimp in me. So I can't really hate you, and there's something infinitely sweet about your entwinement with big Ginny.

Back to our fictional characters. Remember that Bill Alleyn, with
Don's assistance, has asked Linda to the Friday-night dance. The
big night arrives, and faculty chaperone Don watches the couple
all through the dance. A glutton for punishment, Don then offers
to drive them home. (Bill, consistent with his virtue, lacks wheels;
his father drove him and Linda to the dance.) It's crowded in Don's
Karmann Ghia, but Don likes it that way, with Linda in the middle.
They stop for refreshment at the Europa. Mike Allota walks in with
some buddies, insults Linda, and spills water on Bill. Bill floors
Mike with two hard punches. I'm telling you: the Europa was a
dangerous place. Don then delivers the young couple to Linda's
house and waits in the car while Bill walks her up the steps.

At the front door, Bill tells Linda, "I like you a lot." Then:

**She tipped her head back. He kissed her, but she had never been
kissed in quite this way before. There was tenderness, respect, and
warmth in it, but passion and lust were missing. At first it surprised
her, then she savored that kiss in a way that she had never savored
contact with any boy before.**

A moment later, in her room, alone:

She lay on her back in her bed, staring up into the darkness, trying to recall every look, every gesture of Bill's. She could not remember him clearly, though, for distracting images kept interfering—first of Mike, then Don, then many of the boys she had known intimately during the last two years. Then she thought that perhaps when he found out what she was, he wouldn't want her. She turned her face into her pillow and wept. "Oh, God!" she wailed, her cry a lonely, meaningless sound in the darkness, for she had no one to comfort her, no one to advise her.

Change is afoot. In the car, Bill mentions that he is concerned about Linda's reputation at school. Don replies guardedly. Then Bill probes.

"There's a lot of talk about you and Linda. That you take her out. That you take her to your house when your wife's not home."

Don says nothing. One imagines a gulp heard up and down the Mother Lode.

"Mr. Kaufield, if you've done anything with Linda that, well, maybe you shouldn't . . . I don't quite know how to say what I mean."

"Go on, Bill. I'm listening." Don struggled to keep his voice calm.

"Well, you're sure not doing her any favors. Her reputation was bad enough, I guess. But when they started talking about her running around with you, boy!"

"I think I understand," Don said slowly. Bill had shown him a side of his affair with Linda he hadn't thought of before.

"I hope you do, Mr. Kaufield, and I hope you're not mad," Bill said.

"I'm not angry at all, Bill," Don replied. "There are a lot of things in what you've told me that need thinking about."

This chapter is pivotal in *Campus Sexpot*. Bill Alleyn has shown

Linda a kind of affection she has never experienced before, and he has shined a light on Don's moral center for him. Moreover, the writing in this section is distinctly not bad. The reader's concern with right and wrong rises with the tide of the novel's improved quality and sharpened ethical focus. Righteous energy begins to course through the reader's veins.

But the reader also thinks, *Does this mean no more good parts?*

The facts of life as first told to me:

Source: Alex Neumann, age 11

My age: 11

Place: On the roof of my clubhouse

The Facts: "The man puts his thing inside the woman's hole and goes."

I was appalled, yes, but I accepted it. I knew it would be something like this. But *why?* I had to ask. Why would the man piss inside the woman? Alex said, "Because it feels good."

Around this time, my father, perhaps sensing that the subject was in the air, sat me down for the big talk during an afternoon of hunting. I was eager to get his perspective.

Source: Superior Court Judge Ross A. Carkeet, age 46

My age: 11

Place: Bald Mountain

The Facts: "A lot of boys use a swear word for it, but I don't want you using that word because it's an act of love."

"It" remained hazy. My father provided even less below-the-waist detail than Dale Koby. Instead of practical knowledge, I had gotten only a strong warning about my verbal conduct, a librarian's "shush." During the talk, our dog frolicked near where we sat on the hill cradling our guns. My father said, "Go on, Brownie. You know all about the facts of life." Brownie knew a lot more than I did.

In high school, rumors about sex floated around campus, and I listened to them closely, drawing what conclusions I could:

- When Mary Fraser got naked in Ralph Cunetto's car, he got so excited that he threw up.
- Track star Don Yaney exerted himself so much running the mile that he came into his jockstrap during a race.
- Greg Theall was with a girl in his car, and she had her period all over him, and when he got home that night his father yelled from the living room, "I smell pussy!"
- Eddie Tuttle and a girl at Lake Tahoe buttoned their Levi flies together and screwed that way.

Precious images, to be sure, but they were mere fragments. I needed a panoramic introduction.

The next possible fount of sexual truth, the public school curriculum, was bone dry. In freshman orientation, we learned about common sense in driving and heroin addiction. In a film depicting drug withdrawal, when the addict vomited into his wastebasket, the class pleaded with the teacher to run the film backwards. I was far too frightened to join in the request. I was sure that someday someone would grab me and inject me with heroin and turn me into an addict, and what then?

By far, the most important mode of instruction would be the jokes I heard as a freshman on the wrestling bus, told as we motored vast distances to grope with alien youth in the Central Valley towns of Oakdale, Modesto, Manteca, and Tracy. The jokes were intended to delight, not to instruct, but a young boy searching for truth will naturally draw inferences from tender narratives of the "act of love" such as these.

THE JOKE: Two guys are lost and starving, and they come to a house in the woods. One says to the other, "You wait outside while I go in and see if they have any food." He knocks on the door, and a really ugly woman opens it. He asks for some food. She says he can have all that he wants, but he's got to fuck her first. ("Oh no," we cried out on the bus. "How horrible!") The guy agrees, but at the last minute he just can't do it because she's so ugly, so he grabs an ear of corn from a nearby plate of corn on the cob and sticks it inside her. The woman doesn't notice. ("Right," we thought. "She wouldn't notice.") The guy goes through one ear of corn after another, and he throws each one out the window when he's done with it. The woman finally says, "Okay, you can have all the food you want." The guy runs outside to get his friend and sees him sitting under the window patting his belly. Stripped corn cobs lie all around him. "I'm not hungry," he says. "I'm full from all that hot, buttered corn." ("Eww!" we cried. "Eww!")

THE LESSON: During sex, a woman emits something that is like melted butter.

THE JOKE: A guy wants to fuck a simple country girl, so he says to her, "You like turkey?" She says sure. "Want to make some turkey?" Sure, she says. So he starts fucking her. After a while, she says, "Is the turkey done?" "Not yet," he says. A little later, she says, "Is the turkey done now?" "Not yet," he says. A little later, she says, "Now? Is it done now?" "Yeah," he says, "it's done." "I thought so," she says. "I can feel the gravy running down my leg."

THE LESSON: Whatever the woman emits during sex is plenti- ful enough to run down her leg like gravy. (I now understand that the "gravy" must be the man's semen, but for some reason I associ- ated it with the country girl.)

THE JOKE: A guy is fucking a woman, and she says, "More." So he pulls his dick out and reaches his whole hand inside her. "More," she says. He reaches his arm in up to the shoulder. "More," she says. He puts his head in, then both shoulders, and then he slips and falls inside, where he lands on a sandy beach. He sits up and looks around and sees another guy walking toward him. He says to the guy, "What are you doing in here?" The other guy says, "I don't know, but as soon as I find my car, I'm getting the hell out."

THE LESSON: The vagina is very big.

Sexual education is the subject of chapter 4 of *Campus Sexpot*. The novel leaves Don Kaufield for a while and focuses on three students. Bad seed Mike Allota has dropped in on Linda Franklin at the house of her friend Carolyn, whose parents have gone out of town for the weekend. Mike is hot to trot, but Linda is having her period, or maybe she just claims she is because she is suddenly disenchanted with Mike. So Mike turns his attention to Carolyn, who has been described this way so far in the novel: "goody-goody" (by Linda), "plump, with a figure that suggested a little girl more than a maturing adolescent" (by the omniscient narrator), and "a little too plump and much too immature to interest him" (in Don Kaufield's thoughts).

Carolyn steps out of the room to get some glasses for the sweet Mexican liquor Mike has brought along. Mike says to Linda:

"What about this chick? I've seen her around school, but nobody seems to give her a tumble. She know what the score is?"

"Leave her alone, Mike. She doesn't know anything."

"I might complete her education," he said speculatively. "Specially since you're out of action."

"Mike, she's never had any," Linda said. "Don't do anything to her."

"A real, live virgin. I didn't think there was any of them kind left." He grinned at the thought.

The three adventurers drink. Linda wanders off and falls asleep, leaving Mike with Carolyn. A bit later, Carolyn wakes Linda up.

"What do I do?" Carolyn asked desperately. "Mike. He . . . he wants to do . . . something awful. I'm scared."

"Go ahead," Linda suggested, thinking that it was time Carolyn learned something about the facts of life.

"Go ahead?" Carolyn said miserably. "I don't know how."

"He'll show you. Mike knows all about that sort of thing."

It's a given of this book that women know nothing about sex until a man teaches them — the valley seducer taught Linda, Mike will teach Carolyn. But who taught the men?

THE JOKE: A guy is fucking his girlfriend, and she says, "Deeper." He's already in all the way and doesn't know what to do. "Deeper," she says again. So the next day he jacks off for hours and makes his dick grow to ten inches. But that night it happens again. His girlfriend says, "Deeper." The next day he jacks off all afternoon and gets his dick up to two feet long. ("Wow!" we cried. "Two feet!") And that night? "Deeper," she says. So the next day he gets up before dawn and really goes at it, jacking off all day, until it's five feet long. ("Wow!") That night he says to her, "Is that deep enough?" She says [garbled, suggesting a large object intruding into the mouth from inside], "That ought to about do it."

THE LESSONS: (1) Jacking off can make your penis grow; (2)

the vagina connects directly with the mouth. The second lesson, of course, was part of the joke, and most of us got that. But what about the first lesson? Why didn't anyone in the bus question the premise of growth through masturbation? Because each of us, I am sure, was quietly contemplating the implications for his own behavior. Just what we needed—a new reason to masturbate.

Now comes a very important wrestling-bus joke, one that changed my life.

THE JOKE: Two little boys are sitting on the curb jacking off, and one says to the other, "How come a dick has that big knob on the end?" The other one says, "To keep your hand from slipping off."

THE LESSON: Masturbation consists of a stroking motion along the shaft of the penis.

But, you ask, isn't this coals to Newcastle? Isn't knowledge of how to masturbate innate? If it is, I must say that the hard-wiring in my brain got crossed. I needed this joke.

The first time I tried it, when masturbation talk was in the air but without instructive detail, I swung my member in an up-and-down motion as if I were driving a nail with it. After several minutes, I frowned over my work station. I had achieved an erection, but nothing more. Something was clearly missing. This was no more satisfying than the erections I had had in my poison-oak-plagued days. Two or three times every summer, my crawling around in the woods would result in a bright red body that itched maddeningly for a week. The contagion nearly always included my genitalia, and the arousal from my scratching and rubbing led me to the hypothesis, with the certainty of a medieval scientist, that poison oak caused erections. (Poison oak has been the bane of many in that part of California. An early gold miner on his way to the diggings fell asleep in the midst of a stand of it and was so poisoned that his swollen eyelids blinded him, and he had to feel his way from Stockton to Sonora—a distance of sixty miles. His journal makes no comment about genital involvement, but we may assume the worst.)

The joke about the function of the penile end-knob lifted me out of ignorance. The night after I heard it, in bed, under cover of darkness, I tried the implied technique. To say that I got positive feedback is to understate what I experienced. What happened was that a herd of wild horses began to run wild in my groin, all thundering forward with the intention of charging out and tearing my bed to smithereens.

I stopped short, astonished. A visual examination was called for, so I turned on my bedside lamp and lifted the covers. Lo, there appeared on the tip of my penis the flaring nostril of a single white stallion on the verge of charging, with no doubt hundreds more snorting behind him. But I would not give the command. How could I possibly go on? I was barely fourteen, an undersized tyke, and there was no provision for wild horses in my bedroom.

I turned off the light. It was not a particularly noisy lamp. Still:

"David, is your light on?" It was my mother, calling from the living-room couch on the other side of the wall, two feet away.

"No, Mom."

"It's too late to be reading. It's bedtime."

"I'm not reading, Mom."

"Good night, then."

"Good night."

People talk about the guilt of youthful masturbation. In my case, *fear* is the word—fear for the obvious permanent damage I was doing to my body. It was not possible that I could do this thing that would produce the horses without my body falling apart. All my life to this point had consisted of being in the dark about huge dimensions of life and then suddenly finding out about them, and this was no doubt one more. There must have been a Path to Death that everyone knew about, or at least a Path to the White Stuff, and if you went down this path, your body fell apart.

But the pleasure center will triumph. There came a point—and it surprises me that I don't remember it, that I can't summon it back—when I just kept going and let the horses out, whipping them enthusiastically. I do remember vowing never to do it again, then doing it again as soon as possible. By this time I must have moved my work station into the bathroom, for I don't recall messing up any sheets. My mother would have spotted them instantly. (Kids have no laundry secrets. Once, years earlier, when I pooped my underwear at something funny my brother did, I removed them and took them into the backyard and threw them with all my might into an oak tree. Three minutes later, while I was inside being good, my mother said, "David, why are your underpants up in the tree?")

I must have used the toilet for my private pleasures, though I don't remember it. I do remember using the bathroom sink. I knew that masturbation simulated sex and that sex took place with the man lying on top of the woman, so naturally the sink, set in a surrounding countertop tiled in pink and lavender, seemed ideal for sexual congress. But first I always had to remove my mother's many trays and bottles of lotions, soaps, and perfumes and set them on the wicker hamper lid, one by one, careful not to clink them against one another. By the time I had developed this painstaking routine,

I must have grown comfortable with masturbation—must at least have decided that it wouldn't kill me. But it would have been nice to have been spared that period of terror.

Something like this, perhaps, to conclude my Bald Mountain sex talk:

"Go on, Brownie. You know all about the facts of life. Now, Davey, there's one more thing I want to tell you about."

"What's that, Dad?"

"It's called masturbation. It's also called jacking off, jerking off, beating off, pounding off, and whacking off. Everybody does it, so of course you will do it. Even married people do it. I recommend the toilet—don't worry, your imagination will easily take you to more pleasant, though highly improbable, contexts."

"Do you ever use the sink?"

"That's disgusting, son. Now, here's the procedure. I'm only going to say this once, so listen carefully."

Yes, it would have been something.

Let's go back to the Friday-night dance for a moment. I attended every one of these after-game affairs over a four-year period, but I never gave any thought to the faculty chaperones or their conversations. I should have, judging from the evidence of *Campus Sexpot*. Don Kaufield and a colleague, Paul Skell, share the duty on this occasion, and Paul gives us a glimpse of his world-view. He's worth a listen.

"If these kids ever knew how to dance," Paul remarked, "they've forgotten it."

"It doesn't look like anything I'd call dancing," Don replied.

"Fornication in a vertical plane," Paul said. "Get 'em a little closer together, lay 'em down, and we'd have to call this something besides a dance."

Paul on Linda Franklin:

"Hips made for the act of love," Paul muttered, "and ideally designed to accommodate a pair of hot pants. If she's a virgin, I'll donate half my salary for this year to a home for wayward girls. I've spent my life being interested in girls with hot pants. I've studied

them from every angle. I believe I know all the symptoms, and Linda Franklin has them."

Paul Skell is based on Paul Skilling, my Freshman English teacher. I know this from the similarity of their names and from the physical description when the character is introduced: "Paul was short, stocky, with steel-gray hair cropped close to his head. He wore a vest and jacket every day of the year, regardless of the weather." This captures Skilling perfectly. A walking narcotic, he would tug at his vest, close his eyes in ecstasy, and intone, "The prefix 'arch' means 'chief': an *arch*angel is literally a *chief* angel." I knew no archangels. None of this had anything to do with me. Skilling induced sleep, but he also succumbed to it. As DeMolay advisor, he regularly nodded off during our somber rituals.

Skilling didn't voice any of the fruits of his hot-pants research in Freshman English, so the accuracy of Koby's portrait is an open question. But considering that Skilling made a living saying, "An *arch*angel is literally a *chief* angel," I can appreciate the need to ventilate at the end of the week. The more important question is what did I feel as a fifteen-year-old, when *Campus Sexpot* hit town? The words Koby attributed to a character who had been my teacher would have forced me to entertain the possibility that the apparently high-minded Paul Skilling, walking lexicon and DeMolay "Dad," had enthusiastically entertained low thoughts.

To understand my youthful reaction to this portrait, we must enter the DeMolay chamber. What is DeMolay? you ask. According to the official literature, the International Order of DeMolay "opens doors for young men aged twelve to twenty-one by developing the civic awareness, personal responsibility, and leadership skills so vitally needed in society today." But according to me, DeMolay is a religion without a god. It is ceremony with no object of reverence other than reverence itself. It is a regimen of enforced dignity for boys at an undignified age, and the primary engine of uplift is a vast body of ornate ritual that reads like the Boy Scout oath as revised and expanded by Samuel Johnson.

Astonishingly, DeMolay worked. Twice a month, I watched unruly yokels of doubtful piety play grab-ass in the Masonic Hall locker room as they rifled the closet for robes, and, minutes later, march upstairs and file into the ritual chamber like a stern legion of Supreme Court justices. Heavy on the shoulders, black with a satin sheen, trimmed in red and tied at the throat with a golden braid, the DeMolay robe made it nearly impossible to be a jerk-off.

The meetings would open with the recitation of the chapter ritual, with each officer speaking lines from memory. Although the ritual's Latinate vocabulary and long sentences were a challenge to us, I recall few stumbles and almost no prompting from the sober Masons on the sidelines. (Although never identified as such by headquarters, DeMolay is a junior Masonic organization in its ideology and supporting sponsorship—likewise for its sister fellowship, the International Order of the Rainbow for Girls.) After the ritual came the business part of the meeting, devoted to the DeMolay dance, the DeMolay car wash, the DeMolay regional convention. Did we do good works? Maybe, but I don't recall any. We were preparing to do good works—in the balanced prose of the ritual book, "striving to be better sons, that when we reach the years of manhood we may be better men."

The ritual insinuated itself even into the business meeting, which would run along smoothly until—what's that? *Gong, gong, gong* . . . Ah, yes. The nine o'clock interpolation. At 9:00 P.M., the junior councilor would whip out his hidden gong and pound out nine sober peals, no matter what was happening in the meeting. Even if DeMolay Dad Paul Skilling, floored by an excess of lust in his heart, was receiving artificial respiration, nine o'clock meant that the gong must sound. Silence would descend by the third peal. Perfect peace was upon the assembly by the ninth. Then spoke the master councilor:

> Brethren, at this hour all over our land, mothers are bending over the beds wherein lie the children they love. Also at this hour, guests in institutions are preparing for the hour of rest. Let us pause a moment in our deliberations while the chaplain offers a prayer. DeMolays will kneel on left knee, all others will remain standing.

This is the only sizable portion of ritual from the literally thousands of words I memorized that I can recall in its entirety. And what a passage it is, what a picture it paints. The mothers bending over the beds, the "guests in institutions"—what tension between those two words, what a peculiar collocation, chosen more for euphony than meaning—"preparing" (brushing their teeth? sighing with regret?) "for the hour of rest." The strangely beautiful passage honors the sacred concept of . . . *bedtime!* Of course! The mere thought of bedtime positively makes you want to prostrate yourself in worship. But that was the essence of DeMolay. You never knew what you would be reverencing next. It's a rather early bedtime too, now that I think about it. Those "guests in institutions" were more likely preparing for the hour of *Bonanza*. Words penned for an agrarian nation.

DeMolay felt ancient, but it goes back only to 1919, when a Kansas City Mason named Frank Land supervised meetings of some local boys who had begun to gather for companionship.

Many of them had lost their fathers, as, in a sense, Land had at age twelve when his mother fled with him across the state, leaving his alcoholic father behind in St. Louis (a flight theme that would be repeated, for a while at least, in my own life). Initially, nine boys gathered under the direction of "Dad" Land, as he came to be known. When the number grew, Land called on a fellow Mason, Frank Marshall, to compose a creed to guide and inspire the boys. Marshall, a newspaperman and a fair poet, fashioned a symbol system couched in language that would exercise an almost hypnotic effect on subsequent generations of young male memorizers. Many famous Americans trail robed glory from their youths in the DeMolay heyday of the middle half of the twentieth century: Walt Disney, John Steinbeck, Red Barber, John Wayne, Chet Huntley, Walter Cronkite, Pete Rose, Bill Bradley, the Smothers Brothers. In 1969, if I had made the secret DeMolay sign of distress on the moon, DeMolay Neil Armstrong would have known what to do. If I ever meet Brother Dan Rather, I will slip him the secret DeMolay handshake. And on the night before he resigned, when DeMolay Richard M. Nixon asked Henry Kissinger to pray with him, did Dick do the DeMolay kneel?

Here it is: left knee on floor, right foot forward and flat on floor, right elbow on right knee, forehead resting against right palm. In keeping with the medieval European roots of Masonry, the DeMolay kneel is an accommodating position to assume if you are about to be beheaded, but it is supposedly modeled on the way George Washington prayed at Valley Forge. I remember lots of prayer from this kneel, but no vividly imagined God. There was certainly no Jesus, though it was a Christian Bible that sat on the altar in the center of the chamber. And in the endless traipsing required by the ritual, passing between that altar and the master councilor's station was forbidden *if the Bible was open*, necessitating frequent round-about travel. The people who write to newspaper advice columns asking about proper disposal of American flags are largely former DeMolays cowed by imaginary barriers.

There was plenty of traipsing on the night I was initiated into the order. At the time, the Sonora chapter had such a shaky enrollment that it couldn't put together an initiation ceremony, and our group of fourteen-year-olds had to travel to Stockton, down in the valley, and be inducted by strangers. A membership drive had made our incoming group so large that the usual procedure of requiring all the initiates to walk from one station to another was foregone in favor of one representative to do the marching. I was that one because I was the smallest. My escort, known as the marshal, complained to me after it was all over that I was so short that I slowed the whole ceremony down with my little legs—an ungenerous remark that took some shine off the jewel of *comradeship* that I had just seen the fourth preceptor deposit on the crown of youth.

You see, traipsing along with the marshal and me was another lad, who carried the crown, and the three of us would pause at each station while a preceptor recited a little speech and placed a virtue jewel on that crown—the jewel of *courtesy*, the jewel of *patriotism*, and so on—and then off we went again. Seven stations, and at each one, the crown bearer hit the deck right on cue, dropping to his knee and holding up the crown for the preceptor. The initiation ritual typically went at things the hard way: to walk from one station to the next, we had to make a complete circuit of the room first (Bible status on altar? closed). With each tour, we passed a door that was slightly ajar, and several strange boys leered at me through the opening, sending my bowels into an uproar. I knew without doubt that at some point in the evening I would be conducted into

that room for physical abuse. I was willing to do whatever was required. I just hoped it wouldn't hurt too much.

Instead of that, we were subjected to torture of a different kind. We were given an eloquent and stirring speech about motherhood. The perfect young fellow who delivered it stood before our group and burned us with his unflinching gaze. He told us to take a carnation, a red one if our mother was living, a white one if she was not. One of our group, a classmate, took a white one, and I had no idea his mother was not living. It was a depressing moment. The speaker commanded, "Tonight, tell your mother that you love her. Tell her." Deeply moved, I vowed to do it, vowed with passion. (I didn't.)

DeMolay knew how to grab you, whether with an emotional moment like that one or with a cool detail in the regular biweekly ritual. One of the coolest was the sentinel, who sat outside the closed door to keep intruders out of our meetings—as if people were beating the door down. The sentinel interacted only with the junior deacon, his man on the inside, vouching for latecomers seeking admission. Entrance was beseeched by two raps on the door, known as an "alarm," and granted by two raps. Why two? "To teach those without a twofold deliberation before they seek admission and to teach those within to use double caution before granting it." Damn right. Another cool thing was "the word of the day," which got passed around furtively before every meeting and then would be ritualistically whispered from one brother to another in the chamber, culminating in an official articulation by the senior deacon, a climax on a par with the sudden descent, to blaring music, of Groucho's word-bearing duck on *You Bet Your Life*.

The ritual was heavily *about* the ritual. The master councilor would ask each officer for a brief, stylized job description, going from one to the next via Q & A like "Brother Junior Councilor, where is the station of the senior councilor?" / "In the West." / "Brother Senior Councilor, why do you sit in the West?" This routine bound one DeMolay to another in a network of reference. The symbol system took an overview of life, stressing links and landmarks. The master councilor, in the East, went on and on about the morning; the junior councilor, in the South, was high on the noon of life, when half his days were behind him and half before; meanwhile, in the West, the senior councilor, though his pubic hairs were millimetering forward even as he spoke, mused aloud about life's sunset, when he would happily pack it in, his eye fixed on "the everlasting day" to follow.

DeMolays are usually sons of Masons, though I was not. (My father, a boyhood DeMolay in the valley town of Turlock and a man who never met a gavel he didn't want to rap, would have liked to become a Mason and move through the chairs to leadership, but his application was blackballed by the Sonora chapter for reasons that were never discussed in the house.) Masons come from a wide cultural pool, albeit a Protestant one, and as a result, boys of all kinds groped themselves under those robes. The Sonora chapter drew DeMolays from neighboring Calaveras County, and those kids, coming from a town much like mine and yet all of them strangers, intrigued me and scared me. One afternoon when the Sonora High wrestling bus pulled up in front of Calaveras High, I spied a DeMolay brother standing by himself on the sidewalk. It was Max—more man than boy, paunchy, with a slouching posture and a fixed, slack-jawed grin. I said, "Hey, I know that guy," and, sensing skepticism from my teammates on the bus, none of whom were DeMolays, I piped in my freshman voice, "Max! Max!" He stared and failed to find my face—or, if he did, failed to recognize

me—and, just to be on the safe side, he gave the entire bus the
finger.

Comradeship like this is one of the justifications offered for
DeMolay—not that I demanded one. I never questioned why I
had joined. DeMolay was a closed circle in which, like a character
in a Poe story, I had been imprisoned for obscure reasons. From
my present perspective, it seems as if only the smallest step would
have been required to take me out of that circle, and from that
viewpoint, a mere glance at the pieties would have summoned up
a laugh to shake the rafters. But that kind of thing happened only
later, in college, during drinking nights, when I would discover
that a friend from another town had been a DeMolay, and we would
declaim paragraphs of ritual to each other.

DeMolay taught me two things, one wonderful, the other terrible. The wonderful thing had to with language. Listen to the first
preceptor capturing the queasy transitional feelings of male adolescence as he instructs the initiates on *filial love*: "We have reached the
age when possibly we are ashamed to display the affection that all
right-thinking sons feel in their hearts. We are eager to enter upon
the inheritance of our manhood; yet there is nothing effeminate
in the home-loving, mother-loving, father-loving young man." On
every page, the diction entranced me. In that little book, I engaged
with words that I never saw anywhere else—"enjoin," "emulate,"
"inculcate," and "repair" in the sense of "go" ("Brother Marshal,
you will repair with the stewards") I learned about parallel syntax.
I learned that the relative clause could be my friend. I memorized
the lines of nearly every office in the hierarchy. I memorized the
long public-officer-installation ritual so that I could hear the ladies
say, "Oh, David, you did a beautiful job." I learned the long part of
the master inquisitor—the mean sonofabitch who tortured and

executed Jacques De Molay, a Knights Templar of perpetual obscurity to us, but we knew that he did not betray his friends. In our production, one of our members, a free spirit from up the highway, played the brave, stubborn Jacques, and I, an establishment goody-goody likewise cast by type, tortured and killed this likeable rebel.

What was terrible about DeMolay? For four years I mouthed precepts that I gave no thought to. I looked initiates in the eye and "enjoined" virtues on them that I didn't practice. I embodied Hamlet's advice to his mother: "Assume a virtue if you have it not." Since we all acted righteous and none of us were, and we all knew this about one another, it doesn't quite add up to dishonesty—more like training in future dishonesty. (Arkansas's most famous DeMolay learned the lesson well.) I am struck now by the words of the third preceptor, expert on *courtesy*: "No man, young or old, is really refined who is not courteous and whose courtesy is not natural instead of being artificial and assumed." You mean "artificial and assumed" is bad? But isn't that the whole damn program? Perhaps the founders of the order believed that a virtue repeatedly put on like a robe can become a virtue internalized. But even if true, the steady awareness of falseness takes a toll, making hypocrisy seem the norm everywhere in the world. This parallel dark lesson of DeMolay began right away, at my initiation. During the flower speech, even while being moved to swooning, I thought about the poised lad telling me to love my mother, *What a phony*.

I usually tolerated the discrepancy between DeMolay ritual and reality. I didn't mind that at the state convention in Fresno, boys from all over California conspired to schedule a mass toilet flush in the hopes of rupturing the hotel's sewer pipes. And Chaplain Vaughn Radcliffe's obsession with poker, which he played in his underwear nonstop for three days with like-minded strangers at the convention, was a mere peccadillo. (Vaughn was my first experience of a type of male: born to play poker, more comfortable in that society than in any other.) And of course I enjoyed the Swisher Sweets we smoked through the convention and the *Playboy* pin-ups someone produced and put under the glass of our hotel-room dresser.

But it was hard to overlook this: One Sunday afternoon in my early days in the chapter, just before the public installation of new officers, the incoming master councilor took several of us aside and produced a cellophaned condom from a pocket under his robe. It was my first rubber, right there in the holy of holies! He snorted a few times and said he planned on putting it to good use after the ceremony. Our eyes went to his date, a blank-faced innocent perched on a folding chair in the front row. I didn't think that she had ever gone out with the braggart before, so his prediction was probably wrong. More important, what about the seven cardinal virtues of the initiatory degree? What about *courtesy*, which included "courtesy toward all women"? What about *cleanness* (we were to foreswear "the cheap vulgarity of unclean jests")? It was as if a staggering drunk were wearing the crown of youth, and the jewels were dropping off it left and right.

So when I read *Campus Sexpot* for the first time and saw DeMolay Dad Paul Skilling rendered as Paul Skell, when I saw him reincarnated as an English teacher who talked not about archangels but about hot pants and his lifelong study of them "from every angle," was I shocked? Why would I have been shocked?

What is a small town? Let's turn to the local newspaper for an answer—the *Union Democrat*, est. 1854. We'll pick a date and see what tendrils the stories send out. January 4, 1962, is a good one, for in that issue's Campus Letter, written by the newspaper editor's teenage daughter, we find the first public discussion of our subject:

> Dale Koby, former Sonora High English teacher, has written a book, "Campus Sexpot." It is the most talked about literature in school. You could make a fortune by selling copies of it for $10 or more, because there aren't many available and everybody wants to read it. Characters and settings are taken, without much change, from SUHS. Everyone wants to know if he's in it.

The editor himself will have more to say about the book in the next day's paper, but let's see what else there is of interest in this issue. Right next to the Campus Letter is a report of some main-street hubbub. A car with a jammed accelerator crashed into the display window of a clothing store, and "a mannequin was knocked from its feet and fell over the front of the car, prompting some

spectators to call for help for a man they believed had been pinned
by the car." This happened at Calvert's Store for Men, the very place
where I fusspotted over snap-tab shirts and stifled murderous im-
patience while customers failed to make up their minds, employ-
ment I recall as a two-year coma that turned *me* into a mannequin.
I wasn't there for this mishap, but Police Chief Ron Wano was,
according to the paper. Ron was my pony-league baseball coach, a
soft-spoken man who would hang his sidearm on the dugout fence
and methodically hit ground balls to us through one-hundred-de-
gree July afternoons, oblivious to the sweat blackening his blue
police uniform.

A story on page 5 of this same issue hits closer to home:
"DeMolay Mothers Elect Officers" announces the bold headline;
the landmark event occurred "at the Ross Carkeet home on Meyers
Hill," where "Mrs. Carkeet was named decorations chairman." If
contemplating life as viewed from the dizzying heights of DeMolay
mothers decorations chairman has you panting for more, consider
this item from the same issue: "The SUIIS Dixieland Band will
play for the Fireman's Ball tonight. Members of the band include
Stan Moe, David Carkeet . . ."

What is a small town? A small town publishes a newspaper that
makes the reader feel comfortable. On a typical day, it's about people he knows and places he's been. On a good day, it's about *him*.

Twenty-four hours later, in his regular column titled The Sierra
Lookout, the newspaper editor weighed in on *Campus Sexpot*. It
was a tricky column to write. "What's your Koby-name?" he begins,
quoting a question often heard on campus, thanks to "a former
English teacher who arrived in a goatee and left a year and a half
later without the goatee." The column gives the Koby names of
several faculty in the book without identifying the originals, but

everyone in town could easily do that. The sexual content of the novel is never directly broached, only implied by the book's title and the word "potboiler" to refer to it. The editor claims not to have read it. "My information is incomplete and second-hand. The book isn't available locally and most of those who have found it on out-of-town book racks say they haven't been able to finish it." The innocence of the village has been largely preserved. He concludes, "More complete information is available from the publisher: Art Enterprises, 8511 Sunset Blvd., Los Angeles 26." Sonorans didn't want "information" from Art Enterprises — they wanted the damn book. The editor managed to facilitate its acquisition without seeming to encourage the reading of it. Clearly he was the smartest man in town.

Other items of interest in this issue? At the bottom of the front page, right below The Sierra Lookout, is an ad inviting everyone to sample the "chicken livers or sweetbreads sauteed in Marsala wine sauce" at Pastorini's Longhorn Restaurant. I vied for a girlfriend with this restaurateur's son, Dan Pastorini. I got the girl, then lost her to another; young Pastorini had bigger livers to fry: he went on to become starting quarterback for the Houston Oilers in the 1970s. A few pages into the issue, we find a report on the installation of a new batch of DeMolay officers, and in the accompanying picture, we spy eager little Senior Deacon Dave Carkeet, though as far as photos go, a week later, in the picture of the wrestling team, the caption mysteriously reports, "Sophomore Dave Carkeet, in the 95-pound class, is not pictured"—home sick, maybe, launching Pastorini sweetbreads into the speckled enamel bowl fondly known in our household as "the vomit pan."

And what was Judge Carkeet up to at this time? On January 7, he handed down a guilty verdict in a drunk-driving case. Remarkably,

I didn't know the offender. On January 10, he accepted a guilty plea on a burglary charge from Butch Lyons, age eighteen. Lyons, barely out of high school, had been a classmate of my brother's. I remember, as a young boy, walking to town with Corky and happening upon Lyons in an alley near his house. He was deep in a youthful project that was like my backyard Boy Scout merit badge projects and yet different too. He was about to set fire to a meticulously constructed tower of wooden matches, all surrounding a little green army man, whose aggressive, bayonet-thrusting stance looked rather pathetic under the circumstances. I observed the fiery execution, looked at Lyons's broad forehead glowing in the flames, his freckled cheeks, his really quite handsome features, and thought, *This is the face of evil.* Many years later, when I mentioned the incident to my father, he said, "That's interesting. I sent his father up for arson."

A few days after the Lyons burglary plea, the paper reports on the judge's interesting treatment of an escaped and recaptured prisoner from out of town. The prisoner, while being transported from one facility to another, simply walked away when the incompetent deputy in charge of him stopped en route to attend to some personal business, leaving the police car unlocked and the prisoner unrestrained. "He practically invited him to escape," lamented Judge Carkeet, publicly rebuking the lawman. And, by way of acknowledging that the prisoner was, after all, only human, the judge handed down no punishment whatsoever for the escape.

What is a small town? In chapter 1 of *Campus Sexpot*, when Linda Franklin waits outside for her first ride home with Don Kaufield, he is surprised to find her standing right next to his Karmann Ghia. "I know all the cars here," she explains, and we certainly did. A four-page photo spread in my freshman yearbook treats "Cars on the Campus." Fourteen rods are pictured, along with their extremely cool owners, all guys, of course — Nichols with his '47 Ford, Cassinetto next to his '54 Chevy, Liljedahl and his '56 Merc, Hill with his '57 Ford. Some of them, like Quayle's '40 Chevy, look like getaway cars from a gangster movie. The boxy '53 Dodge my brother drove, even though he was as cool as any of these guys, failed to qualify for inclusion: it was unmodified out of the factory, and — the killer disqualification — it belonged not to Corky but to my mother.

Corky. It's a name I learned to answer to. In a small town, if you have an older brother, everyone calls you by his name because they knew him first. To a young boy gathering impressions of the world he is entering, nothing discourages him about the intelligence of adults more than this repeated blunder.

"Do you want to drag Washington?" Mike Allota says in *Campus Sexpot*, and we certainly did. The single street that defined "downtown" was made for dragging, with natural U-turn spots at each end (the Frosty Shop, the Red Church), both higher than the main drag so that you could gaze upon your miniature cosmos before making your descent. As cars passed, you would wave to everyone you knew, which is to say everyone, and then you would wave at them again on the next trip, as if one of you had just returned from a year's journey around the world.

I used to make a similar circuit, before I could drive, in my mind. As a boy, I would lie in bed and summon the name of every store from one end of town to the other. Up the north side of Washington Street — the J. C. Penney store, where the lady wouldn't sell me a Boy Scout knife because I was too little; the old City Hotel, where I saw a bearded drunk lying in the gutter (I was deeply interested, but my mother shuddered and hurried me along); the Western

Auto store with the annual Christmas bike giveaway (I hoped to
win so that I could immediately give the bike to a poor boy I imagined standing nearby); the Gay Nineties, the Wagon Wheel, the
Louvre, one saloon per block, each with swinging entrance doors,
which I liked to push on and then run away (oh bad, bad boy!);
Calvert's Store for Men once again, where thirty-year-old coworker
Donnie Delaney, a bon vivant bursting out of his Ban-Lon shirts,
would grill me about my sex life as a fifteen-year-old, his questions
a ravaging march all over the female anatomy ("Are you getting
any of this, Dave? No? How about that? Are you getting any of
that? No? You're kidding"); Burke's Shoe Store, where I would swap
tales of retail boredom with a friend who worked there (deep in the
store's cool, earthen basement, he had carved out a napping shelf
that I coveted); and up the street to the bike repair shop run by that
grumpy German, Mr. Vierheller, his store built into such a steep
hillside that you could step right onto the roof at the rear, which
my friends did on parade days in order to throw water balloons at
me when the band marched by. Those are just a few of the stores.
I could name them all, and then back down the south side of the
street—a half-mile of stores, round trip.

When my father walked these sidewalks—possibly on his way
from the courthouse to a Lions Club lunch at the Sonora Inn—he
would tip his hat to everyone he passed. He was the last man in
the county to wear a fedora, just so he could tip it. His hand would
rise to its brim, his head would nod slightly to shorten the reach,
and he would give a tip along with a small eye twinkle. Here comes
someone now, so watch him: the hand, the nod, the twinkle, the
tip. It could drive you crazy. The habit was so ingrained that if he
walked in a city like Oakland or San Francisco, he would give the
tip to strangers, puzzling them with his country blessing.

A small town is a defensively cocky place, quick to brag about its superiority before you can make fun of it. We lived in a gold-rush town! Reminders were everywhere, even in the name itself: Mexican miners from the state of Sonora were the first to pull riches from its soil. On Saturdays when I washed the windows at Calvert's Store for Men, I also washed the plaque on the building saying that it had housed the town's first Wells Fargo office. Nearby Columbia was called Hildreth's Diggings in the 1850s, and friendly Ken Hildreth grinned at me from the far end of the trumpet section in the 1960s. Another schoolmate, lucky to be alive in an unusual sense, was a direct descendant of George Donner, leader of the Donner party; George and his wife, Tamsen, didn't make it, but their children did.

We were cocky about our elevation too. Borrowing glory from the Sierras, which reach to over fourteen thousand feet, we fancied ourselves mountain people despite our modest foothill elevation of eighteen hundred feet. Our name for outsiders — "flatlanders" — is common among vain mountain folk, but we had a special name for the outside world in general. If someone said, "She married a guy from down below," we instantly knew what that meant about him: not one of us, different in a way that ruled out full mutual understanding, and why would anyone live down below anyway? The locator applied to towns in the valley, the San Francisco Bay area, and points south all the way to L.A. On one occasion, a Sonoran who learned I was living in Indiana asked how I liked it "down below."

Linda Franklin does not use this expression in *Campus Sexpot*, but she does use another Sonoraism, showing that Koby picked up a few of our habits in his eighteen months among us. Rebellious Linda is no town booster, and early in *Campus Sexpot*, she says to

Don, "The kids in school here think the world begins and ends in this little town. They're content to go to the show on Saturday night." At the time when she speaks, there were two movie houses in town, so you would expect her to say "go to *a* show," but in Sonora one would always "go to *the* show." For many years there was just one theater in town, called the Uptown Theatre—always the elevation brag!—and "go to the show" stuck even after another theater opened at the lower end of the main street.

One of the first movies I saw at the Uptown was *High Noon*, which was filmed partly on location in the scrub-oak countryside around Sonora and in small towns a few miles away, Columbia and Tuolumne. Some of my brother's closest childhood friends appear in one scene, playing outside the church where the marshal—Gary Cooper—fruitlessly seeks the townspeople's help in the expected showdown at noon. During filming, the movie's casting director visited our elementary school and plucked these lucky third-graders from the classroom, bestowing film immortality on them. Lowly kindergartners like me, who put in most of the day looking at Mrs. Dawson's legs from nap-time floor mats, were not candidates for greatness, nor were eighth-graders like my sister, who resented the privilege perversely given the third-graders. (Her only consolation was a glimpse of Grace Kelly at a restaurant in town.) Pity even more the third-graders not chosen to go with their classmates, like my brother. Apparently it was boys with long or messy hair who were chosen, so he can blame his casting failure on my mother and her enforcement of—to use her favorite encomium—the "clean-cut" look in her boys.

In a small town, enmity accumulates, a fact that *High Noon* captures well. Coexistence is an essential art in such a place: if you see your enemy every day, you can't very well treat him like one.

Instead, you display a noble civility. My father showed his mastery of this skill most notably with the Jordans, our neighbors across the street. They were important to me because their tubby dog was on permanent loan to our family. Brownie was fed by the Jordans, he slept there, and he was covered by their medical plan, but every morning after breakfast he would trot across the street to play with us or, on hot days, to sleep on the smooth concrete of our covered front porch. One night, however, I discovered that the Jordans were the enemy.

It was election night, and my father had challenged an incumbent judge who hadn't been challenged in thirty-five years. Success was uncertain, even doubtful. The Jordans had invited my father's opponent and his supporters to their house for an anticipated victory celebration. The nature of the gathering became obvious to us as we watched the cars gather. Even I, just nine years old, knew that scheduling such a party right across the street showed appalling taste. As the evening wore on and it became clear from the radio reports that my father would be the victor — by a two-to-one margin, it would turn out — the cars began to slink away from the Jordans' house. My brother and I tracked the departures through the window, identifying the would-be revelers by name for my father's many supporters in our house. My father disliked his opponent — I knew this even though he rarely revealed such feelings. When the loser and his wife backed out of our neighbors' driveway and their car got stuck in a ditch, my brother and I threw hoots of ridicule into the dark street until my mother pulled us away from the window.

My father never said a word about that party, neither to us nor, I am sure, to the Jordans. He continued waving greetings across the

road as cheerfully as ever. He was generous and large hearted. He
also liked Brownie an awful lot.

There is a quietly moving scene in *High Noon* that to me is a
snapshot of my father's professional life. It shows the marshal,
alone at his desk, sorting through his badges in anticipation of the
posse that will never arrive to help him. It is the portrait of a man
laboring without complaint on behalf of others. In Sonora, when
the townspeople saw that the light was on in the courthouse long
after hours, high in the third-floor chambers, they knew that the
judge was working toward a thoughtful decision about someone's
life, a decision that would admit as much kindness as the law allowed.

When I saw *High Noon* at the Uptown Theater, I saw it with my
father. It is the only movie I remember seeing with him. I was so
deeply stirred by the marshal's perilous solitude that afterward I
felt the need to choose my words of comment very carefully. As we
crossed Washington Street to our car, I said, "He had a lot of courage." My father said, "He sure did." I was six years old. "Courage"
was a new word for me, and I was glad I had used it correctly.

Campus Sexpot seized my youthful imagination because it was one of the few dirty books I got my hands on. Good boys are limited to the smut that falls into their laps — or the smut that they spy in their brother's Chinese chest, known as the "opium chest" in the family, though only he and I knew what it held. I remember just one magazine from his stash and only one item in it, titled "Beauty on the Beach." A photo essay of sorts, it showed a woman lying naked on her back, with sand covering her in three places. That she was on a beach heightened the impact. I went to the beach with my parents — to Pacific Grove every Easter break and to Santa Cruz in August. The beach was something that I knew about. It was easy to install myself in the picture, there beside this woman. Just to be there — think what it would be like! For the few minutes that I held that magazine, it was all I wanted in the world. Yet I knew that anything like it was an eternity away.

Around the same time, when I was in the seventh or eighth grade, I read a typescript novella, thirty single-spaced pages or so, about two women who compete to see which of them can acquire the smartest outfit without spending any money. Each attires herself by having sex with salesmen and managers of clothing departments. They shop in department stores, not in little dress shops like Sonora's Mode O' Day, so it was a big-city tale. The novella told one woman's story, then the other's. The men, without fail, are willing. One of the women is deemed the winner, and her prize is to receive all the pleasure she can handle from the other woman. This surprising coda didn't puzzle me, at least not too much, because it was presented mechanically: the loser "did" the winner, with no mutual attraction or affection, at least in my reading. But it was all certainly uncharted waters. When I returned the manuscript to my brother, he was still with his friend who had somehow acquired it

and brought it by the house, so I must have read it in one alert sitting. They laughed at my boner, evident against my pajama pants.
From my present perspective, the main thing that strikes me is that
I could walk all the way through our L-shaped ranch house, from
one end to the other, with an unflagging boner.

The trash we read as kids stays with us—the characters, the
words. The unresolved questions about technique and anatomy
linger for decades. When *Campus Sexpot* came into my hands forty
years after being out of them, as an experiment in memory I explored what I could recall from the book before opening it. I wrote
down all the names I could remember:

Mike Allata
Linda Franklin
Merkovich
Stoper
Pomo Highway

Don Kaufield's name failed to make the list, but I got all of these
right, though misspelling "Allota." I then summoned up what plot
I could and wrote it down:

Mike, a cruel, dashing fellow, hot to trot, knocks on Linda's door
(house? bedroom?). She doesn't want to do it—why not?—and
says through the door, "I'm not dressed" (or "I'm naked"). And
he says, "Why bother? You're just going to get undressed again
anyway." Cruel laugh. She lets him in. He says he wants to take a
shower. My reaction as a kid: Why would he take a shower before
sex? Wouldn't he want it after sex? I would.

Mike's not dashing, so I misremembered that, but he's certainly
cruel. We are told this so often that it's no wonder I retained it.

As for the scene in question, in chapter 9 Mike indeed knocks on Linda's front door. Here, from the novel, are the actual words that more or less stayed with me for forty years.

"Just a minute," Linda called. "I've got to put some clothes on," she lied.

"Don't bother," he called coarsely. "You'll just have to take 'em off again." He laughed an evil laugh.

The shower memory actually derives from a scene with a different girl, five pages later, where Mike says, "I'm goin' into the bathroom, and take a quick shower. When I come back, you better be ready for me. I want a good piece, understand?"

My recollection of the story, while oddly selective — a single frame or two from an entire reel — was fairly accurate. Why would I recall these moments rather than a sex scene? Because they involve people, they are specific, and they are mean spirited. As for the sex, well, who's going to remember "They were as one, blood pounding rhythmically together," or "She sought nothing from him but surcease from her own passion"?

I remember only one other published sexy novel from my younger days, but I remember it well. The hero is a driving instructor for adults, and he ends up steering most of his female students into the sack. But we also see the drudgery of his work — an honest narrator, I remember thinking. When our hero has sex for the first time with one driving student, she's very excited, so he deliberately slows everything way down. What does this mean? I wondered. What would happen if he *didn't* slow everything down? (We remember not the good parts but the confusing parts.) Near the end, after the hero gets beaten up badly for some reason or other, as he gets into bed with the woman he truly loves, she says that because of his injuries, they'll have to make love slowly and carefully — the way they'll make love when they're very old, she adds sweetly. I fell for that. We long for the human touch, even in the riot of a porn fest.

I didn't own this book for long, but while I did, my friend Alex happened to spend the night with me. He shared my bed, so we must have been pretty young. After I fell asleep, he read the book in one long sitting. I hope that's all he did.

Outside the genre of smut, I was a catch-as-catch-can reader as a boy. I didn't catch very well, and no wonder: not a bookstore was to be found within fifty miles of town. There was only the Sportsman and Burns' Cigars, general stores of ill health where tobacco, beer, and candy were sold, along with a few magazines and paperbacks. Burns' Cigars went up in smoke years ago, but the Sportsman still stands on Sonora's central corner, with its bifold wooden doors and long vertical sign listing the wares: "Cold Beer, Knives, Guns, Ammo, Supplies, Gifts." In these stores I bought my first books.

I bought To Hell and Back, the memoir of World War Two hero Audie Murphy. I remember just one thing from the book—a Hispanic soldier in Murphy's outfit calls the Germans a word I'd never heard before, "sonsabeeches." It was a short-lived acquisition for me. When I tried it out on my mother, she ran to me as if in rescue, her hand raised to cover my mouth.

I bought and read Hot Rod by Henry Gregory Felsen. The hero of this book had the manly name of Bud. Bud was a philosopher of driving, at least until he wiped out in his red convertible. He didn't believe in ever slowing down. His creed was "When you get in trouble, use your head and drive your way out," which my brother fiercely embraced from atop his J. C. Higgins bicycle, shouting out the name "Bud!" as he careened down the steep hills above town and crashed into oncoming cars.

I bought and read *The Kid Who Batted 1,000*, a novel about a boy with the uncanny knack of hitting foul balls. In every at-bat, his coach directs him to foul off one strike after another until the worn-out pitcher finally walks him. So how does he bat a thousand? (A great title; the question nags at the reader.) On the last day of the season, the kid rebels against the coach's manipulation, and by making a slight adjustment in his swing, he hits a ball that nicks the fair side of the foul pole, then clears the fence for a home run. With one swing of the bat, the boy achieves statistical perfection and independence from an autocratic adult. It was the best book I had ever read in my whole life.

I stumbled onto *The Kid Who Batted 1,000*. How does a boy pick a book? He doesn't have a clue. I regularly went to the city library, a one-room structure, long and skinny as a train car, and the chief engineer was Pearl Soulsby, aged, perfumed, powdered, always alone, and always emerging from the bathroom at the rear, where, it was said, she kept a bottle. My sister had worked at the library before escaping to college, and Pearl had just two things to say to me: "How's Carole?" and "Have you read *Freckles*?" I remember this book, by Gene Stratton Porter, as the portrait of a young man at one with nature who builds twiggy little abodes in the forest. It gave me the creeps — a quintessentially sissy book.

Later I found out there were two libraries in town. In addition to Pearl Soulsby's collection of *Freckles*, there was the county library, whose vast, stately stacks I didn't discover until late in high school. By then I was doomed. It was too late. I kept going to Pearl Soulsby, kept telling her how Carole was. That other library was an alternative fate, an intellectual fortune that had slipped away from me. Many years later, Carole explained to me that bad blood from a feud of some kind kept our family away from the county library.

Kids end up reading what's around the house, so the popular books of their parents' generation have a delayed second impact, a boomlet. A house title that intrigued me for years was *Zotz!* a 1947 novel written by Walter Karig. It's about a man who acquires psychokinetic powers. It all starts with a fly, as I recall—the hero points at a fly and discovers he can control it. When my father saw me reading *Zotz!* he chuckled. I asked him why, but he just chuckled. Toward the end of the book, the hero makes a pass at his girlfriend, but it doesn't work because his powers have made his touch sizzling, or electrifying, or something like that. The judge thought that was pretty funny, I guess.

As I neared high school, I discovered the literature of fear. My 1950s equivalent of Stephen King was a collection of horror called *Zacherley's Vulture Stew*, a paperback with a cover illustration of grisly animals boiling in a cauldron. But most terrifying of all was my heavy reading in a genre that I hope no longer exists — gang literature. Evan Hunter is the only author I recall, but there were others, and they wrote about city toughs who brawled and raped their way through life. One sordid tale began, "A plastic bag is a perfect murder weapon." Plastic garment bags were fairly new at the time, as was awareness of their danger, especially to young children. The hood-narrator of the story is a delivery boy for a dry-cleaning store, and he likes the look of one of his customers, a young mother. He extorts sex from her by threatening to suffocate her toddler, which he would never really do —the narrator tells us this so that our strong affection for him won't be diminished. The story ends with the mother turning the tables by tying him up and cinching a plastic bag tightly over his head. "Yes," the tale concludes, "a plastic bag is a perfect murder weapon—and I ought to know." Not a dead man's narrative, exactly; more a moribund man's narrative.

Gang literature taught me that the world was not a safe place. I peopled my little town with gangs, finding likely candidates for membership in the harmless louts who slouched outside the Gay Nineties saloon. I became a Johnny-Stay-at-Home, as my brother called me, afraid that if I showed my face in town these thugs would drag me under the Sonora Creek bridge and whip me with chains.

Relations between the sexes were strained in gang literature. In a story called "Walk Away Fast," two hoods knock each other sense-less through most of the story until they realize that a girl they're both enamored of has been pitting them against each other and cheating on them to boot. They track her down, punch her out, dump a garbage can over her head, and *walk away fast*. It was sto-ries like this that taught me respect for women. This one prepared me for my treatment of Marcia Labetoure, whose bosom, you'll recall, I related to inconsistently. Thus at the end of prom night, I knew what to do: accompany her to the front door, spin on my heel, and *walk away fast*.

Rape was a staple of this genre, but not as it occurs in real life. The rapes I read about were light in violence and cavalier about emotional consequences for the victims. In one story, after a cop saves a woman from a gang rape in a park, he has consensual sex with her right on the spot. It seemed perfectly natural to me since she was nearly undressed already. "Rape" was a new word to me, and in this and other stories, it was so much like sex that I had to ask my brother if "rape" meant the same thing as "fuck." Contributing to my ignorance was the joking treatment sexual assault frequently received. A paperback book called *Pardon My Blooper* was all the rage at the time—a collection of cartoons illus-trating broadcast mistakes. In one of these, the announcer, intending to say "Rug and Drape Shop," said "Drug and Rape Shop." The illustration showed a leering pharmacist, with mortar and pestle, chasing a screaming woman through a drugstore as he mixes a prescription.

In all the time I lived in Sonora, no rapes were reported or rumored in the town or the county. I never heard or read of an accused rapist coming before Judge Carkeet. Yet surely in a town of twenty-five hundred, and in a county of fourteen thousand, over an eighteen-year period, someone was raped.

One summer afternoon near Phoenix Lake, I was helping a friend and his dad, a surveyor, shoot some property lines on a back road. The mosquitoes were bad, but I didn't mind. To a Sierra teenager, surveying was the coolest possible career. It took place outdoors; it involved mysterious instruments and the appearance of higher math; and the surveyor's word carried weight: *Let this be the corner.* As we worked near the road, a clunker zoomed by with three or four guys in it and just one girl. I watched them pass, and I realized that the boys were all going to have sex with the girl. I knew it for a certainty. She seemed willing—she smiled and waved at us, rather like a bride—but I feared for her.

This happened not long after my first reading of *Campus Sexpot,* and a scene in the book—a scene that I find disturbing still today—probably colored my interpretation. It begins with Linda phoning Mike because she needs to talk to him about something.

Mike answered the phone. "Mike's Cat House," he said. "Where quail tail's for sale."

"You're impossible, Mike," Linda said.

"True enough, chick."

They make arrangements for him to pick her up that evening, but when he does:

They drove to a frosty shop on the edge of town, where Mike's three buddies climbed silently into the back seat.

Mike says he needs to drop them off somewhere, but he drives deep into the woods.

"This is the spot," he said. "Perfect, ain't it?"

"Yeah," said one of his buddies. "Like rightsville."

"What . . . what are you going to do?" Linda asked nervously.

Mike explains that she must pay for the beating he suffered from Bill Alleyn at the Europa after the Friday-night dance.

"You're going to make it up to me and my buddies. And I'll bet you can guess how." He grinned an evil, lecherous grin, made more horrible by the deep shadows cast by the dim lights from the dash.

"I won't," Linda snapped fiercely. "I won't. You can't make me."

"I think you will," Mike said. "There are enough of us to make sure that you do. You guys get out my side," he ordered. "I got firsts."

"Lucky bastard," said the first boy as he got out.

"Hurry up, Mike. I got sloppy seconds," the second boy said.

Linda tries to talk Mike out of it but fails.

Mike was soon ablaze with passion, but for the first time in her life, Linda experienced nothing. Watching him in the near blackness and feeling him paw her, Linda hated him, hated all boys and men who sought her only as a sexual object. She vowed that this was the last time she would allow anyone to touch her until she married.

"Listen, bitch," Mike said. "You give my buddies some, or I'll knock you silly, understand?"

She nodded mutely. Mike left the car, and the next youth crawled in and began pawing her. She swallowed hard to keep back the tears.

Later, torn both physically and emotionally, she stood weakly be-
side the car.

"Not bad, huh, baby?" Mike said.

After Mike roars off with his buddies, Linda walks down the road to a distant general store to telephone for help.

When, during our surveying in the woods, I saw that girl and those guys, I knew that at best hooligan serial sex was about to happen. At worst, there was this possibility: although the guys knew they were going to have sex, maybe the girl didn't know it. And if she didn't, would she be free to decide one way or the other? I can't remember who the guys were—they are as anonymous to me now as Mike's unnamed buddies. I don't know who the girl was. I have no idea what happened that day. What I saw in that glimpse—the clunker zooming by, the cheerful wave—is all I really know.

9

There is no teaching in *Campus Sexpot*.

This surprises me since Koby evidently worked hard at it. Many former students remember him positively, talking about his classroom enthusiasm and his knowledge of literature. On one weekend he drove a group of seniors to U.C. Davis for a reading enrichment program, so that they could hear university professors lecture on Henry James and Joseph Conrad. One student who was sick for much of the term gratefully recalls Koby delivering assignments to his bedside. But the teaching profession merits just two mentions in *Campus Sexpot*. In one, the always upbeat Paul Skell challenges Don's claim to having 180 students by saying, "You've got three or four students. The rest are logs." And back in chapter 1, we learn that Don spent most of his first day "organizing the classes that trooped in with alarming regularity every fifty minutes." "Trooped in," "alarming regularity"—not bad! Good sentence number five.

Koby taught juniors and seniors. My brother was his student for a year; evidence of their contact is to be found in a remark Koby scrawled in the faculty photo section of my brother's yearbook, "Carkeet, wake up!" I was a freshman in Koby's final half-year at the school. I must have passed him in the halls and seen him chaperoning dances, but I gave him no thought. I did not have the privilege of hearing firsthand his dispensed wisdom, like "If at first you don't succeed, suck eggs!" I didn't see him remove the American flag at the front of the classroom and replace it for the hour with a Confederate flag. I didn't get to witness his pranks, like this one: In first period, a student who assisted the office staff went from room to room and collected absence slips, which teachers attached to a metal hook just inside each classroom door, a placement allowing the assistant to reach in and, unseen herself, remove the slip; one day Koby, agitated by the impersonality of this daily transaction, attached a rubber-band booby trap to his slips that flummoxed the assistant and brought her into full view of the laughing students.

None of Koby's former students recalls the goatee mentioned by the newspaper editor in his column on *Campus Sexpot*. But a friend of my brother's wrote in his yearbook, "I know we'll never get another beatnik for a teacher." Perhaps some beat vocabulary made it into the Koby classroom. Slang from the movement strangely colors the speech of one character in the book, Mike Allota. From his evil lips we get "chick," "doll," "baby," and "man," and you'll remember frowning when one of his hood buddies called the woodsy location chosen for raping Linda "like rightsville." A later Koby novel (yes, there would be more) contains an ensemble of verbal bongos; one of its San Francisco characters gives this appraisal of a woman entering a bar: "Holy Vishnu. Like, man, way out. Way, way out."

Koby's selection of Sonora High colleagues for inclusion in *Campus Sexpot* has the randomness of viral contamination. A few characters, like Harold Stoper and Paul Skell, are rendered in a way that couldn't have pleased the originals. Others get a joking or harmless mention, but even those must have asked, "Why me, Lord?" I've touched on my football coach, Bud Castle, onstage for just a few sentences as Bud Bastille, "a broken-down softball pitcher." Another is Pete Marinovich, my husky, no-nonsense, big-grinning wrestling coach. (In a yearbook page featuring favorite expressions by faculty, he is credited with "I ain't got no sweat, you candies.") As Coach Merkovich in *Campus Sexpot*, he appears only to break up a fight between two unnamed boys brawling over bragging rights as to who last enjoyed Linda Franklin.

I'm glad, for her sake, that Mrs. Borelli received no Koby name. She was my French teacher for two years, a woman who looked slightly starchy with her erect posture and bunned-up graying hair, but she had a way of warming up a room. Her stateliness made her the natural choice as faculty advisor for the Tall Girls' Club. She was also the advisor for a scholarly club I presided over in my junior year, and we would meet after school to plan activities and trips. At the end of the year, when it was all over, she said, "David, I want to commend you on the *marvelous* job you've done." Something about her words gave them power; they lifted me up a level from where I had been. Her French class I remember as boring—is there a foreign language class that isn't?—and I skipped it so much in my senior year, claiming extracurricular demands because of my hot-shot status, that when I did attend and tried to hide in the back row, at the beginning of the hour she would always exclaim and rain *bienvenues* on me, declaring to the class what an honor it was to have me there in light of my many accomplishments—"David joue de la trompette, il est président d'association d'étudiants"—words that from anyone else would have been entirely mocking but from her were only partly so.

Mrs. Borelli was married to a lean faculty member whose long stride gave him an authoritarian air that made him a perfect ref and ump, which he was at every level, from Little League to high school. He was an expressive, rough-edged drafting teacher, and no doubt many thought the two of them made an unlikely couple. But I think their pairing says something about her completeness as a person.

Most teachers are developmentally neutral. We get a little knowledge, we spy a few quirks, and we move on. But a few reach us with a special message about our worth. Mrs. Borelli did that for me with her glow of approval, perhaps even of affection. In my junior-year English class, Mr. Wilkins did it in a different way.

I mentioned this class earlier—it was where slick dresser and bad boy Allen Cardwell delivered his pell-mell but excellent oral report. The subject of that report, and of much of our writing, was Ole Rølvaag's *Giants in the Earth*, a saga of wretched immigrant farm life on the upper Great Plains that had no obvious connection with our lives. Every week—every day, it seemed—Mr. Wilkins gave us highly specific study questions to write about. He used a plus/check/minus grading system, with a circled plus signaling extra distinction, and my papers kept coming back to me with that mark on them. He was new to the school and didn't know me, and the almost anonymous nature of our communication inspired me. I wrote like the devil, and he rewarded me with a circled plus and a few wry words. Once I accidentally typed a *v* for a *c*, yielding "vommit suicide," and I left it that way deliberately to see what he would say. He wrote in the margin, "Might be interesting."

I had taught myself how to type the previous summer, and one day some students wondered aloud if the fact that my answers were typed, unlike all of theirs, inclined Mr. Wilkins to grade me favorably. He addressed their concerns forthrightly, saying, no, no, he was aware of that danger. "I'm not grading the typing," he said. The class responded with some skeptical but good-natured noises. The general mood was too positive for any real discontent. Everyone was fascinated with the book, with Mr. Wilkins's study questions, with Mr. Wilkins himself—a loner who drove a VW bug and wore a skinny black tie that ended well above his waist. "It must have got caught in a meat cleaver," Gary Murton used to say. Murton worked with his mom at the Purity, our downtown grocery store, so he knew about meat cleavers.

As part of his daily wardrobe, Mr. Wilkins wore a button with a "ban the bomb" symbol (known as the peace symbol only later). In October of that year, during the Cuban missile crisis, he said that he found Kennedy's objection to the installation of Russian missiles on the island hypocritical. "It's no different from what the United States has been doing for years with its missiles in Turkey, pointed at the Soviet Union." We barely understood what he was saying; we just wanted him to stop, not because we disagreed but because we feared something might happen to him if he kept talking like that.

That was the only political comment he ever made. Class was all literature, all Ole Rølvaag. But then something else happened. I started cutting up. I can't remember how, exactly, though I do remember one incident. I threw a wadded piece of paper out the tall, screenless window, and it rattled around the frame for a while, like a basketball circling a rim, before dropping down. The noise brought the attention of the class—and of Mr. Wilkins—right to my desk.

"*David!*" Mr. Wilkins said—a gasp of surprise, but with pretended severity mixed in. He would do that, play with roles, his expressionless face really making you work to figure out where you

stood. (He reminded us of a penguin, partly because of the black
tie against his white shirts, but also because of that unreadable
face.) He ordered me to go get the paper—to everyone's delight,
the typist was in trouble. Our class was on the second floor, and
I knew that fetching the paper would expose me to stares out the
window from the classroom below—Miss Parli's regimented geometry class, pining for distraction—so instead of going outside I
loitered in the hall downstairs for a few minutes and went back to
class.

"Did you pick it up?" Mr. Wilkins asked.

I gave him a penguin face of my own.

"Did he?" Mr. Wilkins asked Gary Murton, who had scooted his
desk over to the window so that he could be a lookout.

"Nope!"

"*David!*"

Back down I went. I picked up the paper. The geometry class
stared at me. I looked up at Murton. He grinned and waved. A
few months later, I would defeat him in the race for student body
president.

On another day, when I made a wisecrack of some kind, Mr.
Wilkins commented before the entire class on my evolving behavior. "David, it's very curious. You were quiet at the beginning of the
year, but lately you've become . . . omnipresent." That was a recent
vocabulary word, and the class liked the way he had hauled it into
service. I said nothing. I couldn't really say what I felt: *Thank you
for letting me experiment with the full range of human behavior.* In
my family's system, one was either all good or all bad. I had been
straining against the rigid categories, I now realized. Mr. Wilkins,
in an offhand, unknowing way, had expanded the world of allow-
able behavior for me.

Mr. Wilkins was Dale Koby's replacement on the English faculty. I doubt that the pornographer would have served me so well.

Mr. Cannon, our band director, though barely thirty, came to us with a past trailing smoky clouds of glory. He had played trumpet in the Chicago CBS-TV orchestra and had had his own swing band under the name of Puff Cannon. This was written on the music stands we used in the school dance band, not ordinary metal stands but nifty two-piece board units that broke down for the road, with cigarette burns and what I hoped were liquor stains on them. He shared his music with us too, which was not conventionally printed but was in manuscript form. I remember the first time the dance band got together— a select group from the whole band, gathered on an afternoon for reasons we didn't understand. Two hours later, a crowd of students had gathered around us in the band room, thrilling to our "In the Mood."

No one was as thrilled as I was. Mr. Cannon, deeply biased in favor of his own instrument, often declared that the first trumpeter was the most important player in any band. These words made me cocky when I needed it—and when I didn't. I was star of the pit orchestras in school productions of *Where's Charley?* and *Damn Yankees* and a frequent soloist at band concerts, able to tighten throats with "Trumpeter's Lullaby" or raise a smile with "Wah Wah Blues."

Mr. Cannon knew the classical repertoire and lifted us up to it instead of lowering it down to us. In addition to yawn-enforcing English suites and audience-pleasing novelty numbers—my father was a real fan of "The Typewriter Song"—we played Debussy's "Afternoon of a Faun," Shostakovich's Fifth, and something by Darius Milhaud. During our first run-through of themes from Stravinsky's *Petroushka*, Mr. Cannon stopped the band right after

a snare-drum section, frowned at his score, and said to Stan Moe, two years my senior and first trumpet at the time, "Famous trumpet solo right there, Stan. It's missing in our version. I'll get it to you tomorrow." He did, from where I had no idea, and Stan played the hell out of it.

Mr. Cannon was always feeding us special stuff. A few years later, on the bus going to the California State Fair, he sat down beside me and said that he'd gotten an urgent early-morning phone call from a fair official requesting a trumpeter to play retreat as soon as we arrived. He had written out the score for it—a fifty-nine-note salute to the lowering flag, which for some reason had been scheduled for midday at the fair. My trumpet was in the bowels of the bus, but I studied the music and imaginatively played it all the way to Sacramento, feeling like a student of Professor Harold Hill's instrument-less method of instruction. I wanted to do well, mindful of the bugler's recent blunder at JFK'S gravesite in Arlington Cemetery (the poor devil boo-wawed one of the notes of taps) and Mr. Cannon's comment on it the next day ("inexcusable"). At the fair, when I coordinated my playing with the crisp flag ceremony, I hoped that the members of the color guard were thinking, *Who is this kid?*

Mr. Cannon was the most fully human of my teachers. I say this in part because I saw him the most and knew him the best. But also his behavior was clearly imperfect. He smoked in front of us when other teachers lit up only in the basement or the teachers' lounge. Once, when a bunch of us were gathered in his office, we were aghast to see him fish a cold butt from his ashtray and relight it. "End of the month," he explained. When he lost his temper at us, we guessed it was because he was hung over. He was mean to the woodwinds in a way that I now know was sexist, since most of them were female. He would isolate a group—"Third clarinets," he would command, raising his baton—and if their playing was particularly listless, he would say, "You look like a bunch of cows waiting to be milked." The trumpeters, all boys, would laugh and laugh.

He was the only teacher I had who told a dirty joke. I remember some older boys being present and getting it better than I did, so I'm guessing I was a freshman or sophomore at the time. It went like this:

Some scientists have been in the jungle for a really long time, and they're getting horny. (I remember our nervous giggles at that word: *Where's he going with this?*) They hit upon a solution—they'll have sex with the female gorilla they've captured. They tie her to a post and one of them gets in position, but then he says he can't do it, she's just too ugly. One of them has an idea—put a bag over her head. They do this, and the scientist and the gorilla start going at it. It turns out to be pretty good. The scientist gets worked up, and so does the gorilla, more and more, until they're both panting like crazy, and finally the gorilla tears loose from her ropes and throws her arms and legs around the guy. He shouts, "Take it off! Take it off!" and the other guys say, "Which? The arm? The leg?" and he says, "The bag! I want to kiss her!"

The joke confused me completely. First, "horny" meant "homosexual" to me. I don't know if this was a benighted, isolated wrong turn I took in my language acquisition or if all of Sonora High had given the word a regional twist. More important, setting aside the gorilla's ugliness, why would the guy want to kiss her? I had no sense that kissing could be part of sexual intercourse. To me, kissing was the first step *on your way to* sexual intercourse. Why go back to first base when you're already crossing home?

My knowledge of Mr. Cannon's past, dim though it was, com-
bined with my sense of his deep energy and restlessness to give
him a certain heroic stature. Here was this dynamo, this cool
Chicagoan, this butt-smoking bandleader nicknamed Puff, putting
the pursuit of a faster life on hold and staying at school after hours
to paint the band room or to meet with rustic parents to plan fund-
raising for the trip to the Seattle World's Fair.

On one occasion, though, his energy was misdirected—when
he tried to change me. The ideal trumpet face is a pancake, with
the upper incisors precisely meeting the lower ones, but I had a
slight overbite. Such trumpeters are easily spotted, their horns an-
gling down instead of out when they play. In my freshman year,
Mr. Cannon undertook an overhaul of my embouchure, consist-
ing of several stressful individual lessons at school where he made
me play with a thrust-out lower jaw. It was like trying to make a
lefty into a righty. My tone was awful, my airstream gutless. At one
point I broke down in tears—a complete collapse. I lacked the
ability to say what I felt, namely, that he was robbing me of some
essential power—I needed this instrument of pride, of self-decla-
ration—and that he had no right to do this. I remember his arm
around me as I wept, asking me what was wrong, saying I should
tell him, saying, "Don't be such a man, Dave." I never did explain
my tears. We stopped the attempted change, and for the next four
years, I played the way I wanted to play.

He was underpaid and overworked, living in a cramped apartment with a beautiful wife and three kids, and during a lesson one
day in his living room—a good lesson, a good day—I heard him
say to one of his boys who was acting up, "Don't be a boob, Jeff."
He said it with affection. The kid couldn't have been more than two
or three, and I thought it was a terrific thing to say to him.

The teachers that cross our paths illustrate the frightening role that chance plays in our lives in general. I could easily have missed Mr. Cannon altogether. He began teaching at Sonora High in the fall of my freshman year, and he moved away a year after I graduated, earned a Ph.D. in music, and taught at a California state college, where he developed a master's degree specialty in improvisation. I recently reconnected with him after nearly forty years and arranged to have lunch with him near his home south of Sacramento. It was a pleasant meeting, but problematic too. I never satisfactorily expressed the intensity of my feelings for him, perhaps even confounding him with my enthusiasm. For him, Sonora was a five-year interval; for me, it was the beginning of my life. He had been waiting for me in a booth, and as we got up to leave, I noticed that he limped and used a cane. He told me he had lost a foot to diabetes. This seemed like such an injustice that I felt as if the floor had opened and was about to swallow me. He noticed my distress, and he shrugged and smiled. "It's an improvisation," he said.

From kindergarten through several years of university study, I had 108 different teachers. A few were awful, most were okay, a few were stellar. But when I think of these three — Mrs. Borelli, Mr. Wilkins, and Mr. Cannon — I imagine them putting me in a giant slingshot, pulling back on the elastic, giving me a farewell pat on the head, and letting go.

When Bill Alleyn entered *Campus Sexpot* and sprinkled virtue dust all over the place, those readers who asked, "Does this mean no more good parts?" were right to be concerned. Linda's rape in the chapter immediately following her date with Bill is certainly not a good part. In the next chapter, Don's fight with his wife is not a good part. Yes, unfortunately Nelda returns to the story for a brief visit and a long argument, and Don works his pipe pretty hard. Only one character, Mike Allota, is still getting "any," but he can't be relied on, for when he says to the girl he's trying to bed, "Look, bitch, get hot or I'll slap you silly," that's not really a good part either.

It's time for punishment. You can't have all that sex going on in a book from this era without consequences in the end. Linda's penalty was her rape by Mike and his goons. But Linda is just one of three doomed girls. (Justice gives the males in the book a free pass.) Remember Mike's girlfriend, Judy? No? Don't feel bad—the author forgot about her too after chapter 1, but she returns to the novel bearing bad news for Mike: she's pregnant. Mike's resulting freak-out prompts this from her: "You're supposed to ask me to marry you." Mike chokes down this fate, and they break the news to Judy's parents. Judy's father, a new character, has the interesting habit of reacting to bad news by spewing lighted cigars across the living room. He does this twice, in close succession, and it's not clear to me if the second cigar is the same cigar, retrieved from the floor, or a new one. At any rate, Mike and Judy get married in Nevada, and in the hotel room, Mike turns on the charm, saying, "Hurry up and get undressed so I can find out what married tail is like."

The third character earmarked to warn us against sex before marriage is poor Carolyn Stepman, Linda's goody-goody friend. All it takes is one time, as the health teachers always said, and her one sample of bad sex with Mike on the night he "educated" her means that Carolyn too will become a mother. But at this point *Campus Sexpot*, almost as if the author knew what he was doing, takes what appears to be a dumb overuse of a plot idea and makes a serious point about taking control of one's life in a conformist world.

Listen to Linda and Carolyn as they discuss Carolyn's options. (This is before Mike marries Judy; the two girls don't know yet that Judy is pregnant.)

"First, you have to decide whether or not you want to marry Mike," said Linda.

"Marry Mike?" Carolyn said through her tears. "I . . . I guess I do. What else is there to do?"

"Now wait a minute," Linda cautioned. "Don't make up your mind too soon. Mike's a slob, and if you marry him you'll have him around all the time."

"I don't know, Linda," Carolyn cried. "Should I marry him?"

"Just think about what it would mean to have him around all the time."

"I don't ever want to see him again." Carolyn buried her face in her hands and sobbed harder.

As a result of this talk, and with the help of her understanding parents, Carolyn arranges to live temporarily with an aunt in Phoenix, far away from her town's prying eyes. There she will have the baby and put it up for adoption. Good ideas make for good prose. This is from the scene where the two girls break the news to Carolyn's mother:

"You see, Mrs. Stepman," Linda said. "Carolyn's going to have a baby." The silence that followed was a physical thing, and it hurt to exist in it. The sordid story was soon told, and the three women cried together, united in the burden women have had to bear since the first seduction.

And when Mr. Stepman gets the news a few pages later, after Carolyn has already left for Phoenix:

He pulled his wife to his side on the couch. They sat together for a long time without speaking, sharing the closeness that comes from years of living in harmony together. The house was quiet and dark—lonely, too, with a gloom in it much like the gloom that settles on a house upon the death of a loved one.

Finally Mr. Stepman spoke, embodying all of his anguish in a few words. "If it had just been someone she loved," he said.

There is no judgment here, no condemnation of the girl for having had sex. This good sequence of scenes began back with a good question, when Linda asked Carolyn if she wanted Mike around all the time. It seems like a basic question to ask before marriage, but in the *Campus Sexpot* era, pregnancy erased it from consideration. In those days, if a girl got pregnant, she got married, even if the father was the Blob. To have sex meant you would be willing to marry your sex partner—an implied contract whose scariness will be readily apparent to anyone who pauses to imagine married life with a mere sampling of sexual partners from the past. Linda gets smarter as *Campus Sexpot* progresses, and here she has leaped forward a decade in her perspective on teenage pregnancy.

Dale Koby was able to dramatize the options available to pregnant teens because he faced the same problem while at Sonora High—not as a lover but as an advisor. A student—a sixteen-year-old junior boy—came to his house one night with a heavy heart. He told Koby that his girlfriend, just fourteen years of age, was pregnant. The boy assumed they would now get married, but Koby was able to get him to admit that he didn't really want to do this. Nor did the girl. Koby suggested that they put the baby up for adoption, and he took his idea, along with the two youngsters, to the school counselor, who responded with deep, inflexible shock. "I could never be a party to such an idea," she said. Koby argued with her—"The most humane thing for everybody is for them to give the baby up," he said—but to no avail.

The source for this story is a book called *A Teacher Confesses to Sex in the Classroom*, published in 1966, five years after *Campus Sexpot*. Koby's name appears nowhere in the book, but the Library of Congress catalogs him as its author, and many details in the book confirm the attribution: descriptions of the town, the school, and the people, complete with pseudonyms—the autobiographer is a pipe smoker named Del Kendall. You can play *Campus Sexpot* all over again—in a new, revised, nonfiction version.

And I do mean nonfiction. There is no reason to doubt the report of *A Teacher Confesses to Sex in the Classroom*, for it is hardly a self-aggrandizing story. The author tells of trading grades for sex as a photography teacher in San Jose, then of a job teaching high school in a town farther to the south, where he had affairs with two students. From there he went north to Sonora (unnamed in the book), and he tells us that he spent eighteen months in this gold-rush town. For reasons known only to him, when he wrote *Campus Sexpot*, he chose Sonora as the fictional backdrop for his real sexual encounters with students elsewhere.

Unfortunately, like *Campus Sexpot*, *A Teacher Confesses to Sex in the Classroom* has no moral core. The author portrays himself as predatory and manipulative but shows no more contrition than one finds in the Roger Miller song of the period, "Dang Me." He plays mind games with his young charges, his favorite being exaggerated devotion even as the affair is ending, just to see what reaction he can get. While the book is surrounded by uplifting scholarly apparatus — it is published by an outfit called PsyMed Books, and three separate introductions condemn the author's behavior — the detailed raunchy chronicles of seduction contradict the confession's ostensible cautionary purpose. But for all that, the book does have one noble moment: the author's intervention on behalf of those two bewildered students.

That story turned out this way: After the dismal session with the counselor (Mrs. Corporal in *A Teacher Confesses to Sex in the Classroom*, presumably school counselor Mrs. Sargent in real-life Sonora), the kids got married. Koby writes, "Their parents were so ashamed that they refused to have any kind of wedding for them, but instead got the superior court judge to marry them privately in his office." (That would be Judge Carkeel, whose robed appearance in *A Teacher Confesses to Sex in the Classroom* was evidently too fleeting to earn him a Koby name.) The marriage failed, and the young wife left town with the child. Later, on a Sunday afternoon, the boy came by Koby's house for another talk. The author, depressed by the outcome, apologized for failing to help. "You're the only friend we've had," the boy countered. "Nobody else even came to see us. It was like we were suddenly in a strange town, instead of in the town where we were both born and raised."

This description of the town's ostracism makes me squirm. When I was a freshman, a classmate of mine—a very pretty girl—became pregnant and then immediately disappeared, along with her upperclassman boyfriend. It's possible that this was the couple of Koby's story, but I don't know for sure. All I remember is that they vanished. I didn't feel sorry for them—I had no feeling of any kind that way, because I couldn't get beyond the much more mundane and self-absorbed thought that her pregnancy meant that the girl, who was my tender age, had had sex, *had done it.*

After they disappeared, I never thought about the couple (that was the point of evacuating them), but two reminders came my way later. One of the occasions was in Sacramento, one hundred miles distant, as I was passing through on a trip home from college. At a gas station, I suddenly recognized the man pumping gas into my car—he was the father. He seemed not to recognize me, and I said nothing. I just wondered how his life had gone since he had been forced to leave high school. And a few years before that, shortly before my graduation from high school, I was looking through some old photographs with a classmate named Ellen, photos that were taken when we were freshmen, and one of them leaped out at me—it was the girl who became pregnant. "Oh," I said, and I must have stiffened, because Ellen mocked my reaction. "Oh, *her,*" she said, putting into words the haughty judgment of my body language. Ellen was way ahead of her time. I was a perfect representative of mine—the DeMolay master inquisitor, enforcing the moral order.

Bill Alleyn wouldn't have stiffened at the sight of that girl's picture. I say this because after Linda is raped, and after she phones Bill to be rescued and tells him the whole story, including her fear that she might become pregnant and not even know who the father is, he says that he loves her and will marry her if that happens. When I first read *Campus Sexpot*, I don't remember being struck by Bill's goodness. The quality did not interest me then. But now I must say, though he is carved out of a solid block of wood, Bill is good to the point of being inspirational. Koby, inspired himself, draws a lovely scene at this point, the most intimate one in the book. In front of her house, drained by her ordeal, Linda falls asleep in the car, enfolded in Bill's arms. For two hours he doesn't move so that she can sleep in peace.

We are near the end of Koby's tale. In the final chapter, we learn that Bill's offer of marriage will not be needed, for Linda, unlike Judy and Carolyn, is not pregnant. But she has spontaneously decided to see the county juvenile officer and tell him about her affair with Don. Meanwhile, Don has blurted out to Paul Skell that he has had an affair with Linda. Paul, who is really beginning to get on my nerves, silently produces a blank piece of paper.

"What's that?" said Don.

"Your resignation. Write it out, I'll get it accepted by the board over the telephone. I've been warning you all along to leave Hot-Pants Linda alone. The heat of your passion has cooked your goose."

"What can happen if I choose to stay?" Don asked.

"The least they can do is slap a rape charge against you. In this state that's five to ten. They might lynch you if they get upset enough. Resigning is the wise thing to do. It's better than getting hanged for being hung."

Witty Paul concludes with some straight advice for Don to "stop by the courthouse and look in on the situation there." Paul happens to know that Linda has gone to see the county juvenile officer, but this sounds to me like a reason for Don *not* to go to the courthouse. No one eager to get out of Dodge stops by the marshal's office for a final look-see. But the author, sacrificing plausibility to structure, is funneling all his major characters to the courthouse for a rousing conclusion. Bill Alleyn tags along with Linda, and the juvenile officer has also summoned Mike, who is having a really bad day: his cigar-spewing father-in-law just learned that Mike slapped his daughter, and he's out for Mike's head.

Juvenile officer Jim Stember is described as "a stout, red-haired man with a florid face," words that bring Jim Pember right before my eyes. He was the probation officer who worked with kids in trouble, usually in conjunction with my father. In addition to taking in many foster children over the years, Pember had children of his own, and one of these, Ann, smote me mightily just before I went off to college. The song that played all that summer began, "When I woke up this mornin', you were on my mind," and she was certainly on mine. The song brought her to mind so strongly every mornin' that I imagined she was in the musical group singing it. One day Pember, noting that I had been calling on his daughter, said to my father, "I keep a close watch on my kids, but David is someone I know I don't have to worry about." I heard those words quoted to me, and I thought, "Then you're a fool." When, after a day on the river, still in her two-piece swimsuit, Ann kissed me on her doorstep, her body seemed to merge with mine. I had hopes for more but of course never got there, in part because of my undiminished ineptness but also because of her steady boyfriend, whom I had somehow ignored in my calculations. He said to her, "Break off with him, or I'll break him." She delivered this news to me at the Mother Lode Fair, and as she spoke, the song's lyrics faded swiftly into the summer air.

When Don is summoned into Stember's office and sees Linda sitting there, all his sphincters tighten. But Stember says that because she took the initiative in the affair (ladies, be warned), he won't bring charges against Don—exactly *what* charges is not clear. The rape charge that Paul Skell mentioned? If so, Koby has come full circle in his confusion. Remember that a high school was the inspiration for this story—thus the opening-day assembly and the "seniors" in chapter 1. But Koby set the book in a community college and bumped the campus sexpot's age up to nineteen. Since Linda was not forced into having sex with Don, the rape charge makes no sense unless statutory rape is meant, and *that* makes sense only in terms of the novel's genesis, not in terms of the actual potboiler in our sweaty hands. Pity the poor devil who plunked down fifty cents for this book and is thrashing in confusion at this crucial juncture.

Also, let's not forget that Linda actually *was* raped by Mike and his three thugs. Mike's wringing his hands in the hall at this very moment, awaiting interrogation, and the reader fully expects punishment to be handed down, either from the law or from Bill Alleyn's sure fists. After all, when Linda first told Bill what Mike and the others had done to her, he said, "I'll kill them. I'll kill them for making you suffer." But Koby does not follow up on this plot thread. In fact, the only punishment handed out goes to Linda: she gets a two-month sentence and is dragged off by a police matron without the nature of her crime ever being made clear. I've heard of blaming the victim in a rape case, but I've never heard of incarcerating her. Mike is left squirming when the scene ends, his fate forever undetermined in the book. If you visit the courthouse today, you'll probably find him still sitting in the hall.

Don skips off home and calls Nelda, who is down below again, tending her ailing father. Don tells her of his resignation and says he wants to take the family on a trip. Okay by her! she says. (Eldercare gets old in a hurry.) He says he'll bring the kids down and pick her up so that they can all go to Mexico. The reader's last thought? It would have been more fun with Linda.

If *Campus Sexpot* were an experimental novel, rather than ending at this point, it would give us another chapter in which Don Kaufield meets the author of his being south of the border. For that is where Dale Koby went when he suddenly left Sonora.

d, for every Koby-named citizen in its pages, defamation either direct negative portrayal or by association with a seedy context?

Copies of *Campus Sexpot* began trickling into town a year after Koby's departure, in January 1962. Local oral history confers the honor of the Great Discoverer of the book on various competing candidates, former Koby students who had graduated and moved to big cities where such books were found—a rancher's son attending Sacramento State, the former Sonora High Science Club president in San Francisco, the Methodist minister's daughter somewhere else. Recollections by my classmates who read it are foggy about the chain of transmittal: the book was suddenly in their hands. (But one report from a younger alum is quite specific. A mere seventh-grader in 1962, he would first learn of the book six years later, when, in the course of trading paperbacks with Navy shipmates on an aircraft carrier off North Vietnam, *Campus Sexpot* fell into his lap. We can easily imagine his disorientation in those foreign waters to find his beloved hometown so oddly memorialized.) I have no idea how many copies of the book made it to Sonora, nor do I know how my mother obtained the one that she and I read (and I then incinerated). In recent years, for my return to Koby's world, a classmate who is a retired California highway patrolman managed to conjure a *Campus Sexpot* from his basement. His mother's pale signature on an inside page claims first ownership. No doubt a few other copies throb in the darkness of Tuolumne County cellars.

Campus Sexpot did not mark the end of Koby's literary exploitation of Sonora. He wrote *Airborne Passions*, published in 1962, which, according to its cover copy, treats "a new breed of airline tarts, who crave a man at every airport from Frisco to Idlewild," and while little Sonora, with its pathetic private airport, merits no

"Just Wondering," says the headline of a light piece in the S͏o High *Wildcat* of February 17, 1961. Among the whimsical qu͏ tions posed in the article is "Just wondering who's sorry that N͏ Koby left." This could be a lament (*He brought* Beowulf *to life!*) o͏ a Koby-neutral question for the ages (*We pass through this world and no one gives any thought to our leaving*). But most likely it was written with a wink (*How could anyone be sorry? He was a kook!*). Whatever the meaning, it was the middle of the school year and Koby was gone.

Why did he leave? Where did he go? No one knew. Koby gives no reason for his resignation in *A Teacher Confesses to Sex in the Classroom*. He only remarks that a colleague told him that he was headed for trouble anyway because of his "reputation for popping bras of the girls." From Sonora, Koby went right to Mexico, where he wrote *Campus Sexpot* in six weeks. The sole interpretive comment on the novel in *A Teacher Confesses to Sex in the Classroom* is this brain-cramper: "When the book was published, the townspeople were not to understand it the way it was meant." What possible meaning could *Campus Sexpot* have other than sexual excitation direct rendering, the main character is all screwed up because of her domineering father, "the high school superintendent in a small mountain community." This would be Koby's old Sonora High boss, whose welcoming speech to students in *Campus Sexpot* is denounced by Linda Franklin as "crap." We'll never know the full story behind that particular enmity. *Focus on Flesh* (also 1962, a productive year) takes place entirely in Sonora but without any recognizable townspeople in it. The locale is captured in many details as well as in one broad description: "There was an air of antiquity about the town that suggested it had been left just this way by the gold-hungry miners who swarmed in the area some hundred years before."

A nice sentence, but the rest of the book is a mess, as are *Airborne Passions* and yet another novel from this year, *Darkroom Sinners*, set in San Francisco with one mention of Sonora environs. In all these post–*Campus Sexpot* books, stalwart heroes who happen to be excellent cocksmen are menaced by one-dimensional villains acting out of obscure motives. Inspired by the hard-boiled genre, the plots contain mysteries, but they are developed as afterthoughts, and the sex gets in the way, happening obligatorily no matter what else is going on, rather like the DeMolay nine o'clock interpolation. The chief device for advancing the story is not action but constant banal dialogue; the reader of a Koby novel longs to enter it not in order to have sex but in order to tell everyone to shut up.

As for the sex, yes, there is the old *in-out*, but more *out* than *in*, and no wonder. How can you describe sex in an age when the most relevant nouns and verbs for doing so are forbidden from publication? The philosophy of sex that emerges from Koby's depictions is likewise tinged with negativity. Sometimes sex erupts unexpectedly: the devil made them do it. When this happens, it is as if a rushing wall of water buffets people all over the bedroom, and "animal cries" are frequently heard. But planning for sex is bad too, especially if you're a woman; more than one Koby hero is repulsed by a too-lusty female whose frank desires are condemned as "gross." For Koby's characters, sexual desire is an all-consuming craving, and intercourse is a release, a "surcease," to borrow one of the author's favorite words (used eight times in *Airborne Passions*). Sex is like passing a kidney stone or having an urgent bowel movement. *There*, everyone seems to say afterward. *I feel better now.* Perhaps the bleakest single statement is from *Darkroom Sinners*, where the meaning of the universe is "the spasm that provides man with a few moments of peace and contentment in a life spent in fruitless striving."

For a perspective on the Koby hero, let us take a short trip to Seattle—two trips, actually. In the very same months when Sonorans were frowning over their copies of *Campus Sexpot*, they raised ten thousand dollars to send the high school band to the Seattle World's Fair. In early summer, the band went north. It was an eternal bus ride, and eternity is best spent making out, which I did with flutist Cathy Candelrubie, known by the trumpet section as Cathy Can-o-whoopee, but true whoopee was still years away, and we just kissed furiously for twenty-two hours. At the fair itself, we were strangers to each other. She went off with her friends, I with mine.

Or rather, I went with mine until they dumped me for Stella, who was not a band member but rather a nude fair exhibit presented in the guise of international exotica on Show Street, the adult-entertainment section of the fair. Stella drew every male touring school musician on the West Coast who could pass for eighteen. My face could get me into Cub Scouts but not into Stella. I knew it and my

friends knew it, and without ceremony they dumped me. In addition to humiliation, I remember feeling shock at the stampeding
male sex drive on display when my friends stormed the portal to
Stella. I also remember the sad, regretful look one of them gave me
even as he went along with the others.

Disqualified from manhood, I staggered around the fairgrounds
and wept openly, oblivious to what I looked like. If I had run into
another Sonoran, I don't know what I would have said. A while
later, I returned and found my friends outside the Stella exhibit,
hopped up from the show, which they described for me. Stella had
lain perfectly still, revealing as much of herself as the law allowed,
while the crowd stared. She had been so immobile that a question
now arose as to whether she was a person or a mannequin. One of
the group swore he saw her chest move with breathing, and this
was good news to all.

Other groups of Sonora boys saw Stella as well, and they developed a code to refer to her, "bonketa bonketa," which recalled the
drumbeat of the show and also suggested the size of her breasts.
On our way home, as the bus sat hot and stalled in Seattle traffic,
one of the boys became possessed with the memory of Stella, and
he began pounding on the metal base of his aisle seat in rhythm
with his cries of "bonketa bonketa." An algebra teacher chaperoning the trip finally brought him out of his frenzy with an explosive
"*John, stop that!*" The bus moved on, and Stella became a quiet
memory for the boys, something to think about on the way home.
I had nothing to think about. I wasn't with Cathy Can-o-whoopee
but opted instead to sit with the friend who had cast me that sad,
lingering look on his way to see Stella.

Seattle was a psychosexual nemesis that summer, for I returned
with my parents to do battle again. There comes a time in every

teenager's life for a last road trip with the parents, and it's always one too many, and the teen thinks with horror, "I should not be here." That was such a trip for me, sitting all alone in the backseat of my father's Chrysler New Yorker, with no companion except for my random spontaneous erections, plodding over the same highway miles to a familiar destination that I now viewed with distaste, staying in motels with this silent couple who stopped at every gift shop on the road and had no idea what was raging inside me: the very drive that had seemed so shocking in my friends when they had stormed Stella. At the fair, alone most of the time, I discovered a different exhibit, one that fed this drive — a room where fairgoers stood and watched an arty European montage of film clips on all four walls. One brief scene showed a voluptuous woman pouting her lips for a few seconds. She was fully clothed, but I had never seen anything so arousing. I went to the show over and over, just for those few seconds, and I became so charged by them that I considered grabbing a female standing nearby — any female would do — kissing her, and then running away.

This state of perpetual, dangerous sexual agitation is the permanent condition of the hero in Koby's fiction. The author never got beyond "bonketa bonketa."

Campus Sexpot and the three other Koby novels I've mentioned were published under the Epic imprint by Art Enterprises, Inc., of Los Angeles. All are either 158 or 159 pages long. They are published in numbered sequence, and the numbers are high: *Campus Sexpot* is no. 115, *Darkroom Sinners* no. 128, and so on. But the numbers are inflated, since they begin with 101, and it so happens that the title of no. 101 is . . . *Hot Rod*! Surely you remember that legendary philosopher of the road, Bud ("When you get in trouble, use your head and drive your way out"). Judging from this and

other early titles, like the futuristic *1976—Year of Terror*, the series
didn't start out as a sexy imprint, though it certainly ended up that
way. After no. 104, it's all titles like *Passionate Trio, Sorority Sluts*,
and, for fans of dialect in literature, *Lusty Hillbilly*.

Koby reemerges in 1964 as the founding editor of the *Magazine
of Modern Sex*, a journal containing serious-minded articles on sex
in all its dimensions: premarital sex and guilt, group sex, fetishes,
aphrodisiacs, nudism, and techniques across cultures, to name a
few. Like *Playboy*, the journal advocates free inquiry unfettered by
traditional taboos, and it largely lives up to its manifesto. However,
it falls well short of another implied goal, scholarly respectability.
The articles are sketchy, the writing often simple minded.

Koby's name appears only on the magazine's masthead, but he
must have written at least some of the articles in the issues he
edited; "Where Do Sex Offenders Come From?" and "My First
Night of Love" are attributed to Dale Brittenham, and this was
Koby's name at birth. Other possible aliases abound in the tables
of contents. Michael S. Wolfgang and Leonard Lowag, Ph.D., *could*
be real people, but these recurring names show a pattern that appears elsewhere in the Koby record—an English given name with
a Germanic surname, perhaps modeled on names of two real sex
theorists, Richard von Krafft-Ebing and Benjamin Karpman.

The *Magazine of Modern Sex*, like Koby's early novels, came out
of Los Angeles. Its last issue appeared in 1965. The next year brings
us *A Teacher Confesses to Sex in the Classroom*, published in Atlanta,
Georgia, and authored by Robert Leslie, a Koby name possibly inspired by the name of Robert Leslie Bellem, whose lightly sexy
stories appeared in earlier pulp magazines, *Spicy Mystery* and *Spicy
Detective*. The next known Koby product is *The Pendulum Reader*,
edited by him in 1967 and published in Atlanta. This is a collection

of five erotic pieces, some of them reprinted classics, or claiming to be; others are stories with contemporary settings. Koby offers short, rational introductions to each work.

Fans of Koby's fiction patiently awaiting his next novel since 1962 were rewarded in 1968 with the release of *Appointment by Sex* from Sunset Enterprises of Fresno, California. The book depicts one lesbian love scene after another, a strong interest of Koby's, judging from his nonfiction titles of this period—Dale Brittenham's *The Female Homosexual* and Robert Leslie's *Confessions of a Lesbian Prostitute*. *Appointment by Sex* treats a phenomenon I was unaware of when I was growing up—supermarket cashiers doubling as lesbian prostitutes who meet the needs of shopping housewives neglected by their husbands. These cashier-whores ply their trade in the fictional Central Valley town of Heffernan Heights, but, yes, just when you don't expect it, just when it has no place at all in the book, Sonora makes a one-page appearance. A male character remembers it as the town where he and his young bride checked into a motel and had the best sex he'd ever had in his life. Is this a flattering mention? A slandering mention? It mainly feels like a compulsive mention.

From novelist to editor and maybe publisher as well, Koby clearly found his calling: sex in print. In the few years chronicled here, the industry changed radically, yielding more *in* than *out*. In *Campus Sexpot*, the reader will find a mere ninety-five lines devoted to sex scenes—1.8 percent of the total text. Six years later, in *The Pendulum Reader*, the nitty-gritty takes up over half of the book. In *Campus Sexpot*, one finds sentences like "She smiled saucily at him" and "She thrust her breasts up at him with a pert sauciness," but in *Sex by Appointment*, one finds actual sauces, juices, fluids, and the pulsing organs that produce them. While the erotic language of Koby's last books is truer to its subject, it lacks the win- some charm of the clumsy, evasive prose of *Campus Sexpot*.

Koby's collected works suggest he fought an ongoing battle between mind and loins, between his goal of putting real ideas into his books and his competing desire (not just commercial need, but desire) to drown out those ideas with "animal cries" of passion. Among his ideas is a nameless fear, usually of obscure origin and springing from childhood, that dominates his characters' lives and drives them to self-destruction. Manhood, in Koby's work, is a powerful foe of this fear, and it receives special attention in *Campus Sexpot*. Early in the novel, after a nasty confrontation with Mike Allota at the Europa, Don Kaufield's daughter says to him, "Are you mad, Daddee? You look like that man made you mad." Don replies, "That wasn't a man. That was a very little boy." Set against bad boy Mike is baritone Bill Alleyn, and the book repeatedly asserts that Bill's emerging manhood derives from the loving relationship he has with his father. Koby considered this idea important enough to end the novel with it. After Linda has said goodbye to Bill and has been hauled off by the police matron, and after Don has peeled out in his car, Mexico-bound, the book quietly concludes with these words: "Bill turned and walked slowly homeward, planning to tell his father the whole story. The one thing he could be sure of was that his father had confidence in him, and with his father behind him, Bill walked with a manly stride in the world of men."

Dale Koby's print trail ends in 1968. In that year, a former student from Sonora who was in Officer Candidate School at Fort Benning, Georgia, briefly chatted with him in Atlanta. In 1979, Koby died in Los Angeles.

In *A Teacher Confesses to Sex in the Classroom*, when he tells the story of the troubled young Sonora High couple seeking his counsel, Koby presents himself as he must have seen himself—an outsider, an independent thinker not bound by the norms of a backward era, which were especially restrictive in this mountain town where fate had delivered him. In this one instance, at least, it seems a good self-assessment, and it may have been this view of his overall mission that propelled him in his writing career. Something like this—some sense that one is contributing to the world—must partly inform the professional efforts of a person who has shown himself capable of good deeds. Although the products of that career lack merit, there is also the life lived, and who can say what Koby's life was like after he left the classroom? His death may have marked the end of a "life spent in fruitless striving," or it may have marked the end of something better.

Why do I care about this man? In part because he was my first real-life author—he wrote about places and people I knew. But more importantly, he threw me for a loop at an age when everything else was throwing me for a loop. *Campus Sexpot* raised questions I had no way of answering. Is life really as brutish as it is shown in this book? Is sex always like this: passionate but cold? Is there something about Sonora that I don't know that made him set the book in the town? Does he hate us? Was he fired? Did he do it for revenge? The mysteries are less mysterious to me now: Unhappy men write unhappy books; as a novelist, Koby wrote about what he knew, sex and Sonora; as a bumbler, he lacked the ability to anticipate the impact the book would have on the community. That is my reasonable and complete explanation for the entire phenomenon. Nonetheless, even now, all it takes is a glimpse of the book's cover—Linda sitting on a school desk, her breasts falling out as she leans toward a male figure seen darkly from behind—to make me want to cry out again, "Why?"

If you mention *Campus Sexpot* to someone who was a Sonora High student at the time, you will find an immediately engaged listener, eyes dancing with hungry recollection. This is because my generation read the book with children's sensibilities. But Koby's former colleagues shrug the book off, if a little too protestingly. When I brought up the book to one retired teacher still living in the area, he said huffily, "It's been years since anyone's even mentioned it." I have yet to find a single faculty member who admits to having read the whole novel. No doubt the book's publication embarrassed them, but it might have scared them too—some of them, anyway—because of possible scandal. I say this because after high school I would hear of student-teacher affairs that, if the reports were true, took place without my knowledge almost right before my eyes.

In my recent exploration of Koby's life and work, I have watched my interest in him grow to strange proportions. With every rereading, I hoped *Campus Sexpot* would be better than it was the last time. (It wasn't.) As other Koby novels arrived in the mailbox from distant specialty stores, I found myself plunging into their steamy plots while walking back up the driveway, thinking that here he would finally achieve his artistic breakthrough. (He wouldn't.) And as I read them, I realized that I longed for a portrait, however sketchy, of a diminutive, depressed trumpeter, christened with a new Koby name. It takes very little to rekindle this particular child's endless yearning for recognition, even from a dubious source.

Koby also interests me as one who seems willfully to have chosen the dark path. I remember a comment that my father made about a best-selling novel that occupied him on a flight from California to St. Louis, where I lived at the time. He rarely read fiction, so his critical pronouncements had a certain freshness to them. In the novel, a successful lawyer was having an affair with his secretary, and that minor plot point seized the whole of my father's attention. He said, "I don't understand why anyone would complicate his life like that." At the time, I laughed, but now I have a similar reaction to Koby's life—at least to what I know of it—and I pose this question as a cautious man of about the same age and temperament as my father when he puzzled over his text on the airplane: why be bad when you can be good?

It is worth noting here that there is something unusual in *Campus Sexpot*: children. Although there is no music, or food, or television, or recreation, or money, or world politics in the book, there are children in it. Offspring play no role in Koby's later work, and they are normally absent from all noncriminal porn. Yet two gratuitous kids, no doubt drawn from the author's own small children at the time, enrich the book's texture. He wanted to create a fully realized novel, and that intention explains his otherwise unfathomable words about the book, "The townspeople were not to understand it the way it was meant." But the kids become a plot nuisance in *Campus Sexpot*—Don dumps them off with colleague Paul Skell's wife for weeks at a time—and that tells us about Koby's ultimate instincts as a writer and heralds the career ahead of him. But the children in *Campus Sexpot* inspire thoughts of a different possible Koby, one who knew there was more to existence than romping on the rug with a student.

A life can go wrong in many ways, and Koby's illustrates a few of them. In contrast to Koby's life, my father's went right. But my father's life went seriously wrong too, for a time, and it could have stayed wrong. So in his case as well, there is a different person who might have been—a different possible father.

"The boy wants to be a minister and he doesn't give a damn about people." Judge Carkeet handed down this opinion early in my college days, when I was considering this calling. He spoke the words to my brother, who waited several years before passing them on to me. They gave me a jolt even then, all the more because I knew they described me well, at least at the age in question. I wondered about the comment for years afterward. Was it prompted by a passing disappointment and quickly forgotten, or did it represent a deeply held, unvarying view?

It's too bad that Don and Linda and the gang fall short of having to deal with the judge in the final chapter of *Campus Sexpot*. They come close when they're in the county juvenile office—just two flights up the marble stairs of the 1898 courthouse and they would pass through the swinging doors of the courtroom. Or they could continue on to the adjacent judge's chambers. It's a trek I often made, and my visits there had the same feeling from grade school through college and beyond: full of good fellow-feeling but vague in purpose. My father might tell me about a memento on his desk, which was always crowded with them—a small sculpture from an inmate who held no grudge, a drawing from a child he had led through an adoption proceeding. But what then? Although his manner was always relaxed, as if he had nothing but time, I knew that time was exactly what he *didn't* have. Besides, his den of labor always made me feel like a wastrel.

I knew every room in that courthouse. I knew the courtroom, where I watched him as a lawyer in private practice, then as a judge, always poker-faced, always in control. Once I saw him lose his temper as a lawyer on behalf of his client, and a reporter from the paper winked at me to let me know he was putting us on. I knew the law library next to the judge's chambers, where I tried to study on college weekends, the surrounding law books exhaling vapors of dullness that sedated me on the lacquered table. I knew the cupola over the clock. On New Year's Eve, my father would guide me up there with a flashlight from an access point in the jury-room ceiling, through a haunted-house route of ladders and catwalks, until we emerged above the town on the wraparound balcony, where I would take my trumpet from its case and blow "Auld Lang Syne" across the rooftops.

These excursions were a rare personal indulgence on his part, an unusual exercise of a kind of feudal droit. He was lord of the courthouse, king of the county, but he would never have used words like these about himself—would never have even thought them. "Proud" doesn't fit him at all. Nor does "modest," which implies at least an awareness of accomplishment, something he never gave the least sign of. It irked him that San Franciscan Melvin Belli, the first of America's modern wave of grandstanding lawyers, talked up his own Mother Lode roots (Belli was born in Sonora and spent some of his childhood there); my father saw it as a reputation-pumping claim to the common touch.

Dad had the genuine common touch, based on real delight in humanity. My brother and I separately had the same experience many times: some man in town, often a scruffy one, on discovering who we were, would get up close to us, right in our faces, and say with feeling, "Carkeet, eh? Your father saved my ass." That was all we would learn—Dad had saved his ass.

One weekend when I was visiting home from college with the girl I was dating and not scoring with, a Spanish major, my father told us about an upcoming wedding in which he was to officiate. He was worried because the bride, a Cuban, spoke no English. My girlfriend translated the vows for him and coached him through several rehearsals, trying to shape his mouth into pronunciations he hadn't attempted since high school. At the wedding, despite some suffix confusion that led to his declaring the couple "husband and husband," his performance was so successful that afterward he was rushed by much of the Latino population of the county—people who had known him affectionately for years and now were delighted to engage him in their native tongue.

A "Cow County" judge had to have the common touch. That was the name he coined for the association he founded of California judges from rural counties where only one judge presided—of necessity, a well-rounded judge who could handle any kind of case. But one area was his favorite—juvenile law. It was a natural specialty, given how he felt about children. He would let an idle neighbor boy hang around and bend his ear for hours while he dug a ditch in the backyard—company I would find excruciating under those circumstances. In a column in the local paper, written, as it happens, in the very month *Campus Sexpot* hit town, the editor paid tribute to the judge at the prime of his civic career. The occasion was a recent banquet where my father had been the master of ceremonies (one of many such; years later, one eulogizer would say, "For more than twenty years, when anyone else in town got asked to be master of ceremonies, he knew he was second choice"). The column retold many of the jokes my father told at the banquet, like this one:

> Little Billy's teacher asked, "Billy, what are you scribbling in that book?"
>
> Billy said, "A picture of God."
>
> "But, Billy, no one knows what God looks like."
>
> "Well," said Billy, "they will when I finish this picture."

The editor fondly bemoaned the corniness of the jokes and concluded with these words about my father: "We love him—anyway." What I notice now is something that the column doesn't mention. Of the seven jokes reported, five are about children.

Like a child, he enjoyed the little offerings of daily life. Once after pulling into the driveway, he pointed to an acorn on his hood and told my brother and me that it had stayed there all the way up the hill from town. I promptly flicked it off the hood and grinned at him. He liked little observations too. When lined up behind several cars at a red light, as it turned green he would say, "I don't understand why all the cars can't go at the same time." He said it so often that I yelled at him to stop. Once he told us that, presiding over a jury trial as a visiting judge in a San Jose courtroom, he was able to find in each juror an uncanny facial resemblance to some citizen of Sonora. My thoughts: *Must you always be so Sonoran? And shouldn't you have been paying attention to the trial?*

He was a master of the miniature shaving kit, the travel alarm clock, the portable coffee pot. His favorite time, I imagine, was putting these items to use in his motel room, alone, during out-of-town assignments. The judge: his words can put you in jail or set you free, but at day's end, all he wants is a little time to himself in gizmo heaven.

His spirit was essentially playful. Driving my sister and her grade-school friends around, he would sometimes weave in the road to give them a thrill. (My mother hated that; she feared people would think he had been drinking.) If you were sitting in the living room and looked up as he walked by, he would favor you with a goofy smile, for no reason at all, holding it on you the whole time he passed through the room. When taking a break from yard work, he would leave his stiff canvas gloves grasping the wheelbarrow handles, as if an invisible worker were about to wheel it off somewhere. A favorite saying was "The hell ya' beller!" usually thrown at a TV loudmouth. He had a pet name for my mother, "Yahbut," a kind of radio-comedy name derived from "Yeah, but" because she began contrary sentences this way. It mainly appeared on Christmas gift tags — a relic, I sensed, of days when there was more demonstrated affection than I saw around the house.

Among all the fathers I knew, he was the only musician, but he was an unlikely one, with many quirks. Looking too big on the piano bench, he would squint at the notes and puzzle out fingerings on our Acrosonic spinet. He knew nothing of the classical repertoire, losing himself instead in the mysteries of "Mockingbird Hill" and "How Much Is That Doggie in the Window?" His fingernails were unnaturally thick, like hard plastic, and they extended well beyond the ends of his fingers; the clatter when he struck the ivories made it sound as if Popsicle sticks were taped to the tops of his fingers. He was a feeble beat-keeper, and duet partners had to compensate, adding or subtracting time for the sake of unity. Errors didn't bother him — full speed ahead. He served as official pianist for the Elks Lodge, whose rituals required some indoor musical marching that I prefer not to visualize, and he would come home complaining that the lodge brothers cried out, "Take off the gloves, Carkeet!"

An unlikely musician, and unlikely in other domains as well. Any foliage within fifty feet of a cast drew his hook, but he took us fishing. As a carpenter, he was heavy fingered, with a poor eye for design and proportion, but he taught us what he knew, and some of it took: my brother, a college instructor, has built two houses from the ground up. Bad knees from high school football meant he couldn't really run as an adult—he couldn't even kneel without a groan—and a problem with his right shoulder prevented him from throwing a ball with the proper snap. Still, when I was a Little League pitcher, he bought himself a catcher's mitt—as if he needed one against my blistering fastball—and worked with me endlessly after dinner, his knees barking at him the whole time. One of his joys in his sixties and early seventies was throwing the Frisbee because it didn't require him to call on body parts blasted by experience.

An unlikely performer of many skills, but a likely father, born to the task. To his regret, though, he was often absent. During one of my visits home, when my twin daughters were toddlers, I watched him happily hold one on each knee. Later, when he and I were cleaning up in the kitchen, I told him what it meant to me to see them together like that. It made me see, I said—and here my throat tightened, I gagged, the room darkened, I nearly dropped the dish I was holding, I could barely get the words out (I was expressing love for him, you see, probably for the first time)—it made me see how he must have been with me when I was a child.

"Yes," he said—I liked that instant agreement—"but I just didn't have enough *time*." There was something close to bitterness in his words. I couldn't tell if he was cursing fate or himself.

He was right about that, about time. One day I asked him how a car engine worked. He had been walking by my bedroom, and he stepped inside, pulled out a piece of paper, sketched it, and explained it. Spark plugs, valves, pistons, cylinders. Intake, compression, power, exhaust. I went from total ignorance to full understanding in just a few minutes. My main feeling was *wow*. But what stands out now is the singularity of the event.

Could he have carved out more time? Did he need to be out of town as much as he was, or out of the house? Elks, Lions, Eagles, Tuolumne County Historical Society, E Clampus Vitus (don't ask), Boalt Hall Law School Alumni Organization (he served a term as president), Stanislaus State College Advisory Board—were all of these necessary? Maybe they were. As an elected official, maybe he needed to engage with the community. And if he had been around, would *I* have been around, what with DeMolay, band, wrestling, student council, and out-of-town conferences?

But there was another sense in which he was not there. If conversation is a two-way street, he was a road hog. On visits home, his adult children would swallow their own gift of speech at the dinner table and after, when we retired to the living room, because tradition designated him the primary talker. His epic stories of local life would stall repeatedly while he searched his memory to nail down a detail. If anyone else took the floor for more than a few minutes, things fell out of balance until the judge took over with another tale.

Such speakers are poor listeners, not just to your attempts to tell a story but to anything you have to say. If you come on strong with too much detail of a life lived far away, the information seems to daze them. Instead of an active response, you get "How about that?" or, most maddening of all, silence. You want to grab them and command, "Engage with the material!"

Giving measured attention was just one way in which he lived his life at a frustrating remove. He was like someone who is sitting just a little too far away from you, and you long for him to scoot closer. He was not cold, though. In fact he was warm—in gesture, word, and touch. He was just magnificently independent. You sensed a deep contentment, a happiness with himself and with the scope of his life from small to large, and such a man needs people only up to a point. He knew virtually everyone in the county of fourteen thousand and yet had no close friends. When I imagine him at a dinner with colleagues at a judicial convention, I see the others—all men in those days—engaged with one another to a degree that he isn't, as if he is quietly humming to himself.

His religious faith suited him well—Christian Science. He practiced it through daily morning study of Mary Baker Eddy's *Science and Health.* He often went to services in town, telling my mother, "I'm going to m'own today," meaning "my own church," a joking reference that masked the tension in the marriage over this religion. I suspected an early pact between my parents that their children would not grow up in this faith or ever be treated by its methods, and we were baptized Methodist and saw doctors regularly. My father, dwelling in both worlds, was treated by physicians *and* Christian Science practitioners. What better faith for a man temperamentally distanced from others than this one, which believes that the world is an illusion? He operated in our illusory world, even thrived in it and improved it, but all the while he also dwelt in his abstract one. It was something very private for him. Like the little boy in the joke he told, he confidently drew his own picture of God.

Christian Science entered my father's life via his mother, who took it up because of her drinking—she thought it would help her stop, and it did. The Carkeet family tree is heavily decorated with bottles, as far back as recorded history tells us. My father inherited the thirst, and it says something about its awful power that it nearly destroyed the thing that meant the most to him, his family.

His drinking began in college, as it does for so many. (Mom to David, home for a visit: "You're not drinking lots of beer at college, are you?" David, staggered by her omniscience: "That's none of your business.") The role of liquor in his life grew slowly over time, through his marriage and early family life, until it reached a point where his drinking humiliated my mother and caused anguish to my sister, who was old enough to log the results into indelible memory. More than once, stopping by his law office to get a ride home from school, my sister heard an irate client complain to my father's secretary about his sloppy handling of a case. More than once, my mother took my sister on a raid of his office to remove the empty bottles before someone else discovered them. More than once, the police brought him home.

He wasn't an abusive or mean drunk. Just a drunk drunk, but that was bad enough. Sometime early in the fall of 1950, shortly before my fourth birthday, my mother packed several suitcases, called a cab, and took Carole, Corky, and me to Modesto, fifty miles away, to move in with her mother. Carole remembers the ride well. While my brother and I slept in the backseat, she stared out the window at the Big Dipper all the way. But family history is hazy on many particulars. Was my father surprised to come home to an empty house, or had he been warned? What was my mother's long-range plan? What did *I* think?

My father visited us on some weekends, bringing comic books for Corky and me. Carole, always the librarian, created a filing-card system and checked them out to us. According to her, the visits were surreal, since neither the reason for the upheaval nor its likelihood of ending was ever discussed. Only a few weeks into seventh grade at the time, she experienced the abrupt move and transfer to a strange school as a nightmare. I have no idea what I was told about the sudden absence of this warm, affectionate man from my life. No doubt I lived my at-home life and played on the floor with my toys as usual. I do know that forever after, on holiday visits, I found my grandmother's house, with its massive concrete basement, its hot upstairs bedrooms, and its suffocating smell of geraniums planted all around the foundation, neither a happy place nor a sad place. Instead, it was a place where I always felt alert, watchful, expectant.

We stayed in Modesto through fall and on past Christmas. I wish I could say that my father responded to my mother's departure by sobering up, but he didn't. I imagine that he tried to quit and failed. Then, in January, even though there had been no improvement, we suddenly moved back to Sonora—and to a new house. Perhaps my mother thought that a different environment would help her husband turn over a new leaf. Or the house might have been a condition of her return. My brother, in second grade, remembers this as a time of unalloyed joy—old friends back in his life and new playmates in a woodsy neighborhood begging for exploration. Some time in the summer or fall of that year, my father checked into a treatment center near the Bay Area, the Livermore Sanitarium. Of this period the family has a solitary memory: Carole reports that his letters home to her described bunnies hopping on the grass outside his room.

He was sober on his return to Sonora, and he stayed sober, and in that new home I lived a remarkably stable life until I left for college. The town, which knew all about his problem, saluted his recovery and elected him judge five years later. Although the impact of the act was delayed, my mother's decisive step of huddling her children into a cab for a fifty-mile drive, bewildering though it must have been to us, doubtless saved his career, the marriage, and the family. Because he stopped drinking, through all my school-age years I was able to have the father that I describe to you here.

My mother later would grudgingly acknowledge that Christian Science helped him stop drinking, just as it had helped his mother stop. He never talked about it—why he drank, why he stopped. But he did write about it, in a letter to his brother, composed seven years later.

I used to think I was being very unselfish with my family by working hard, spending night after night trying to make more money; never staying home; never sharing family life, etc that I was giving them everything I could in an earthly manner and since I was depriving myself of lots of pleasures that other men had such as hunting, fishing, golfing, etc, I was being unselfish. Oh, of course, I did let myself indulge in liquor, but I convinced myself that that was the only luxury I was according myself and it was all right,—a sort of necessary stimulant to keep on with the grind.

I knew that my steady drinking and getting soused and

embarrassing my family was a canker sore on my family life, but kidded myself into blaming all my loved ones and friends for misunderstanding what a really great and unselfish man I was.

Suddenly one day I awoke with a great sobering thought—and it was a simple one—and it was this: that there surely must be nothing as selfish as a drinking man;—a man who will, for the exaggerated increase in stature he derives from alcohol put his own wife, and children and family to grief and shame. How selfish that a man will lie, cheat,—do anything just to drink liquor and pretend great pretensions and turn his back on such real and permanent things as love, affection and loyalty.

There is no talk here of the power of faith or of the sobering blow of finding that your wife and three children have left you. The sudden insight he talks about, the recognition of one's selfishness, I never heard a word about. And yet its opposite, selflessness, best expresses how he later gave of himself to his family and to the people of Sonora.

It was harder to stop drinking in the 1950s than it is now. Liquor flowed more freely then, and it continued to flow around my father—at parties, banquets, and conventions. My parents gave a Tom and Jerry party for the neighbors every Christmas, and Mom, fretting about the temptation when Dad mixed the drinks, asked me to be with him. "Want a hot toddy, Davey?" he would say, and he would make me one, without the rum, of course, but I would suck on the foam and nutmeg and go help him chat up the nervous guests, most of them in the house just once a year, on this occasion. When I was old enough to drink, if we were out eating pizza, he'd ask if I wanted a beer with it. When the prospect of ordering wine came up at a family dinner, he always said to us, "You go ahead." He didn't want to dull the party. "You go ahead."

And I did. I went ahead. At twenty-one, I discovered bars. So *this* is what adults do, I thought. Not bad! A summer of language school in Europe taught me what was really possible in this realm (nobody gets drunk like German students). In graduate school, drinking threatened to wreck my budget, so I home-brewed and kept my nut down to three cents per bottle. A Kingsley Amis character, tired of fancy ads for alcohol, imagines an ad for his beer if he were a brewer: "Bowen's Beer: Makes You Drunk." The same went for Carkeet's beer. Water, sugar, yeast, and a can of malt syrup. Two weeks from the supermarket shelf to your brain.

It's amazing how it can go on, how you can drink and no one knows, especially if you're a private person and a late-night drinker. Even a family with a history of alcohol abuse will miss it, as mine did when I returned to Sonora for visits. My parents maintained a guest liquor cabinet down low in a nook behind the kitchen table. You could get the door open only so far before it banged into a table leg—just wide enough to ease a bottle out. The cramped conditions, the blind groping, the need to sprawl on the linoleum provided just the right measure of desperate industry to thrill a drinker on a quest. Bourbon, scotch, old rye (my father was the only American I knew who favored rye), gin, vodka, from big quarts on down to little airplane bottles—it was a glorious stash that no one seemed to know about but me. The only problem was that I couldn't drink a bottle dry, for then I would have to dispose of it, and my mother would spot it as quickly as she had spied my soiled underwear in the oak tree. Thus, over many nights spread over years of visits, the bottles became depleted down to the bottom half-inch. The week my father died, I was home for several days, and there came a time when dwindling resources forced the decision: not to drink or to finish off the dozen bottles as a kind of Whitman's Sampler in a one-man, midnight wake.

The next day I found myself in an uncomfortable situation. As we prepared to leave for the funeral in nearby Mountain Shadow Cemetery—so named for Bald Mountain, where my father had taken me hunting and given me my content-free sex-education talk—I noticed that the trash hadn't been picked up from its collection point in the backyard. It was easy to see this from the plastic bags on top of the full trash cans, among them, in fact right on top, the bottle-filled bag I had sneaked down there the night before. My mother said that the truck was probably delayed because of repair work on the main road from town. She went on to say that some local dogs had lately been ransacking her garbage and strewing it all over her yard, and she worried that this might happen during the funeral.

She wasn't alone in her worry. I didn't want my mother to anguish over her son's obvious alcoholism on her return home after laying her alcoholic husband in the ground. With a heart heavy for many reasons, I went off to help bury my father. But Providence favored us, for on our return the trash was gone, the yard spotless. I immediately wondered where that night's drinks were coming from.

I quit drinking on the one-year anniversary of my father's death. I quit because I saw the future. The term "progressive disease" suddenly became as fresh and meaningful as if I had coined it. I saw ruin ahead, and it scared me. I was able to quit earlier in my life than my father—before drinking caused measurable pain to my family—but I could do so only because he quit when he did. Some families pass growing financial fortunes on to successive

generations. In our family, the growing fortune was the sense of
responsibility.

On a subsequent trip to California, my mother and I visited
Pinecrest, a lovely mountain lake where I had spent much time
as a boy with my parents. There, at a picnic table, on a sunny day,
I told her I had quit drinking. "Good for you," she said. She is a
small, almost birdlike woman, but she spoke those words with a
force that made my heart leap. She didn't really know how serious my problem had been, and, in keeping with family tradition,
she didn't ask. My announcement simultaneously declared that I
had had a problem and now I didn't, and that was all she needed
to know. But the relief in her voice declared how much misery
the bottle had brought to her life—and how much it could have
brought to mine. Her last cloud of concern had passed.

No doubt there are at least as many jewels in the crown of inebri-
ation as there are in the DeMolay crown of youth, and my Sonora
family displayed most of them: nameless fear, pathological other-
directedness, hyperachievement, and taboos on the strong statement of feelings. Another one is lying. Drinkers lie about their
drinking and end up lying about everything else. My father, straight
in all his dealings, escaped this particular affliction, at least in rela-
tion to others. His lying took the form of the defense mechanism
of denial in a way that was complicated by his faith. When a spot
appeared on his lung in 1982, he denied that it had the power to
kill him. He made my mother keep it from her three grown children until metastasis brought the cancer into view as a tumor on
his neck a full eighteen months later. It's hard to think of a more
unfair demand one parent could make of another. For years after
his death, I was angry at him for not physically attacking the tumor
in his lung, for doing nothing other than talking with Christian

Science practitioners. Later I was comforted to learn that at the time of its discovery, he was probably doomed anyway.

But denial has its place in life (the previous sentence might even be an example), and I remember a striking instance of it related to my father's condition. When he grew very ill, we moved him into the back bedroom, the room my brother and I shared growing up, because his nights were restless and he and my mother, who was exhausted with the ordeal, each needed a separate bed. One night weeks into the new routine, he came into the living room, the pain just barely under control, and sat for a while. Then he rose to return to bed. But instead of going into the back bedroom, he went to his old bedroom at the other end of the house, not absentmindedly, but with resolve. My mother was awake, her bedside lamp on. I trailed after him, not sure what was happening, and I saw her eyes widen as he eased into his accustomed place beside her. He said nothing, only leaned against the headboard with a pained sigh and looked straight ahead, recovering from his exertions. My mother stared at him from her side of the bed as if he were a stranger who had walked in off the street. After a minute or so, he rose and went back to the sick room. It was the last time he was ever in their bedroom. My mother's response was understandable, given the circumstances. But I can't help thinking of other ways she could have responded.

When I remember our Sonora life, I think of the living room. There we opened Christmas presents, always giving our father the same prank gift, a beaten up wallet with my brother's old blood-caked wisdom teeth taped to it ("Jeez, what a letdown!" my father would say, always fooled). There he and I played the dying game of cribbage ("Fifteen-two, fifteen-four, and there ain't no more").

There we played piano duets ("Let's try 'Country Gardens,' Davey"). And in the living room I said good-bye to him.

I had been visiting from St. Louis, and I had to return home for a while. As he sat in the rocking chair, dying, I bent down and kissed him on the head. I told him I would come back as soon as I could. I squeezed his shoulder and told him that I loved him. He patted my hand and said, "You're a good boy. You're a good boy."

I wanted him to say something else. That he loved me. Or, since I was nearly forty, that I was a good man. I knew that these could be his last words to me—as in fact they turned out to be—and they seemed wrong.

But now I don't question them at all. "You're a good boy. You're a good boy." How could I not want to catch those words, coming from such a man, and hold them close to my heart for the rest of my days?